YOUR ◀
ATTITUDE
▷ COUNTS

Rosemary T. Fruehling
Neild B. Oldham

PARADIGM

Project Editor	**Jeffrey W. Josephson**
Editorial Services	**The Oldham Publishing Service**
Cover Design	**Heidi Libera**
Illustrations	**Heidi Libera**
Composition	**The Oldham Publishing Service**

Library of Congress Cataloging-in-Publication Data

Fruehling, Rosemary T.
    Your attitude counts / Rosemary T. Fruehling and Neild B. Oldham.
        p. cm.
    ISBN 1-56118-073-4
        1. Psychology, Industrial.   2. Industrial sociology.
    3. Interpersonal relations.   I. Oldham, Neild B. II. Title.
    HF5548.8.F79   1990
    650.1'3'019—dc20

                                                                    90-33249
                                                                    CIP

Printed in the United States of America.

10 9 8 7 6 5 4 3 2 1

Contents

Preface

Your Attitude Counts is a nuts and bolts primer in the field of business human relations. It teaches the importance of good working relationships for career success and illustrates how attitude affects human relations. Using an inductive approach, students learn how human relations influences productivity and harmony in a work environment.

Your Attitude Counts can be taught in the classroom or in the workplace. The objectives of this book are performance-based and are accomplished through case studies, exercises, and stimulating questions for discussion and contemplation.

Organization of the Book

Your Attitude Counts contains 22 case studies developed along four general themes.

Case Studies 1 through 5 define attitude and human relations and identify different kinds of relationships that exist in a work environment.

Case Studies 6 through 11 analyze destructive and constructive attitudes in terms of human relations and show their impact on motivation and morale.

Case Studies 12 through 18 concentrate on building good interpersonal relationships.

Case Studies 19 through 22 cover damaged relationships. These chapters suggest strategies and tools that can be used to restore a damaged relationship and look at the consequences of failing to repair damages. The final case study looks at positive ways of leaving a job.

Each lesson consists of a case study and a background section. Students read the case study first and analyze it before reading the background section. After reading the background section, students reevaluate their analysis in light of what they have learned. The discussion section allows students to contemplate human relations problems and attitudes that they have encountered.

The case studies provide a concrete setting in which students can apply their understanding of attitude and human relations. By subsequently reviewing and discussing their first reactions, students internalize the human relations principles.

Study Guide

The *Study Guide* provides numerous exercises and stimulating questions for discussion and contemplation. It also includes a competencies checklist to identify and measure your human relations skills.

Instructor's Guide

The *Instructor's Guide* contains answers to all assignments, suggested test questions, and course guidelines.

Acknowledgements

The authors are indebted to Joyce Anne Grabel of New London, Connecticut, for her ideas and significant contributions to this text. Thanks also go to Carolyn Webb, Robert Morris College, for her comments and suggestions.

Rosemary T. Fruehling
Neild B. Oldham

Case Study **1**

THE NEED FOR
HUMAN RELATIONS

Case Study 1
The Need for Human Relations

After completing this chapter, you will:

☐ Recognize the need for human relations skills.

☐ Define human relations.

Once, in a large city, two women ran for the office of mayor. It was a big city and it had many problems. People of all races and beliefs lived there, as did the very rich and the very poor. Taxes were high, yet the city did not have enough money to cover all its needs. In addition to that, several office holders in the current administration had been forced to resign and some were even sent to jail for theft and corruption.

The city clearly needed a strong leader, one who was honest and capable. Both candidates told voters they were that person.

Donna Mitchell was one of the candidates. She had many skills that a mayor needs. She not only had a law degree, but she was also a trained accountant. She had been a senior partner in a large accounting firm. Furthermore, she had worked for the U.S. Treasury Department in a high-ranking spot.

Beth Gonzales was the other candidate. She had gone to work as a buyer for a large department store chain with headquarters in the city when she graduated from college, and she did not have any advanced degrees or special training. She worked her way up until she was manager of the chain's major branch, which was in the city. She clearly had good managerial skills even if she lacked some of the qualifications her opponent had.

Donna campaigned on the theme that the city needed a professional like her. Donna looked at problems cooly and analytically. She liked to be specific and quote facts and figures. She disdained displays of emotion. She disliked small talk and was not good at it. She said the campaign was about competency and qualifications, not emotions or ideologies. When asked what she would do if lack of money made it appear that a hospital in a poor area would have to be closed, she said she would have to take a hard look at the figures and make a tough-minded decision. Overall, she had a sound plan for improving conditions in the city.

Beth made a point of having been part of the city all her life and having made good there. She was rarely specific and talked generalities. She laughed a lot and liked chatting with people. She said people were what mattered, not facts and figures. She had no specific plans for what she would do. But she listened closely to all the people and made promises to do what she could to help. When asked about the hospital, she said she would do what was best for the people.

Insofar as having a specific plan to improve conditions in the city and the ability to carry it out for the good of all, Donna clearly was the best choice for mayor. The people elected Beth.

Your Analysis

Explain the outcome:

_____

_____

Evaluate the outcome:

_____

_____

Would you change it if you could?

_____

_____

How would you change it?

_____

_____

Concepts

A person can be extremely well qualified, have a lot of technical skills, be honest and hardworking, and still fail to achieve goals in life or be satisfied. A reason for this is that there is virtually nothing that we do that is not affected by how well or poorly we relate to other people.

We All Need Human Relations Skills

When you interact with other people, you are engaging in *human relations*. We all interact with other people. We cannot escape doing so in our crowded, complex, interrelated society. In a single day you relate to co-workers, salespeople, bus drivers, parents, children, sisters, brothers, bosses, teachers, customers, neighbors, friends, postal workers, and so on.

Some of these relations are pleasant, some strained; some unpleasant; some fearful; some satisfying, some not so satisfying. Overall your success and satisfaction in life will be influenced by how well you relate; that is, by your human relations skills.

Human Relations Is Communicating

Because you are involved in some form of human relations practically all of your waking hours, human relations skills are clearly important. Human relations is communicating with others.

That involves obvious direct communication, such as talking and listening, writing and reading. It also includes nonverbal communication using body language, consciously or subconsciously; how you dress, how you take care of yourself. It involves what you communicate and how you communicate.

Being aware of the importance of human relations is an important first step to developing good human relations skills.

Being aware of your own human relations skills is the next important step.

Being aware of these skills does not mean being self-conscious. But it does mean knowing how your actions are received, perceived, and interpreted by others.

Human Relations and Technical Skills Needed

If you believe, as Donna did, that as long as you have the technical skills, your relations with people do not matter, then, like Donna, you will probably lose some important decisions in your life.

This is not to say that if you have no skills at all, you can get by on charm and good human relations alone. Such a person might fool people for a while, but seldom for long. Just about everyone knows a person with no real skills, but with charm, who manages to get along with others doing the work. Such a person is an example of the power of good human relations skills. Of course, ultimately, such a person wears out his or her welcome.

What you need for sustained success and satisfaction is a combination: the technical skills coupled with good human relations skills.

Essentially, good human relations is being aware of the effect you have on others, caring about others, and being sufficiently self-aware of what effect you are having on others.

Review

Consider the answers you gave before reading the concepts. If you feel that you understood the situation and are satisfied with your first answer, write "no change" on the line. If you feel you have new insights or understanding, write your new answer or additional information.

Explain the outcome:

_____

_____

Evaluate the outcome:

_____

_____

Would you change it if you could?

_____

_____

How would you change it?

_____

_____

Discussion

1. In your own words, define human relations.

   _____

   _____

   _____

2. In your own words, explain whether you think human relations skills are important for you.

   _____

   _____

   _____

YOUR ATTITUDE COUNTS

Case Study 2
Your Attitude Counts

After completing this chapter, you will:

☐ Define attitude.

☐ Recognize how attitude affects human relations.

☐ Identify one of your attitudes and how it affects one of your human relationships.

Jane Martin had operated a daycare home for five years. When her youngest son was born, she had quit her part-time job as a drugstore clerk. To supplement the family income, and because she loved children, Jane babysat for her friends.

After a year, she obtained her state license. Jane now had a group of six toddlers she cared for. Her playroom was cheerful and inviting. She subscribed to magazines for parents, read books on childcare and felt well-informed about early childhood development. Jane developed a curriculum of stories, finger plays, and arts and crafts. She included some daily, although she had no set schedule of activities.

Her toddlers were happy, and parents regarded Jane highly. Her friendly, open attitude made it easy for parents to approach Jane with any concerns. They felt comfortable trusting her with their children. Jane had a waiting list of parents who wanted to enroll children in her daycare home.

Doris Buckholz was also a daycare provider. Doris had been an aide in a nursery school before her children were born. When she decided to stay home, it was natural for her to continue to care for children. She applied for her state license, and has been caring for children for seven years.

Doris has an associate degree in early childhood education, but had stopped her studies when her oldest daughter was born. She planned to return to obtain her bachelor's degree when her children were in school full-time. She subscribed to several journals for preschool instructors.

Doris ran her home daycare much like a nursery school with set times for activities. She had specific drop-off and pick-up times and discouraged parents from stopping by during the day. Doris's daycare home appealed to parents who wanted a more academic setting for their children. Doris had regular conferences with parents, but did not exchange small talk with them at drop-off and pick-up time.

Doris considered herself a professional. She hated being referred to as a baby-sitter. She felt daycare providers were underpaid and lacked respect.

This year, the state required daycare providers to attend a six-hour course to renew their licenses. Neither Jane nor Doris was happy about this. They felt that their years of experience and satisfied clients proved their competence.

Jane decided to make the best of it. She told herself that it would give her a chance to meet other providers. She might also pick up a few tips. She arrived with an open mind, and introduced herself to those around her. Jane found the classes interesting. She knew much of what was covered, but her knowledge and experience were valuable and she contributed during discussions. At the breaks, younger providers sought her out. She also learned some new activities.

Doris arrived resentful. She questioned the teacher's qualifications. She believed that there was nothing she could learn. Her education and years of experience qualified her to teach this course, she felt. Doris tuned out the class, did not participate in the discussions, and avoided socializing during breaks. Doris considered the experience a waste of time.

Your Analysis

How would you characterize Jane's attitude toward her job? How would you characterize Doris's attitude?

_____

_____

Is Jane a better daycare provider than Doris? Is Doris a better provider than Jane? Or are they equally competent?

_____

_____

How did Doris's attitude toward the classes affect what she learned? How did it affect the class?

_____

_____

How did Jane's attitude toward the classes affect what she learned? How did it affect the class?

_____

_____

Concepts

Your behavior is affected by your attitude. Your attitude influences the way you look at your whole environment.

What Is an Attitude?

An attitude is the beliefs and feelings you have that cause you to react in a certain way to an object, a person, a situation, an event, or an idea. Your attitudes determine how you interact with others. Your human relations skills can be enhanced by your attitudes, or they can be limited.

Positive Attitudes

A positive attitude makes effective human relations much easier. People respond to an enthusiastic person in a positive way. As a student, you may have found that the classes you looked forward to most were the ones where the teacher was obviously enthusiastic about the subject. The teacher's excitement and interest in the topic were communicated to the class. In the work environment, a positive employee can raise the morale of a group of co-workers.

A positive attitude makes learning easier. Jane was open to new experiences. Her willingness to learn helped her learn new skills and make friends. Her positive attitude also benefited the class. Sharing her experiences was valuable for her classmates.

Negative Attitudes

Negative attitudes limit your ability to learn. Doris's negative attitude cut her off from the class and new experiences. She had valuable knowledge that did not get shared. She also might have learned new things to use in her business if she had been open to them.

Your attitudes have been created over the years by everything that has happened to you, by what you see and read, by your families and friends, and by the social class to which you belong. Your culture and ethnic background influence your attitude. Both positive and negative attitudes influence your developing personality.

But you are not solely the product of your environment. To a certain extent, you choose which attitudes to accept and reject. You adopt the attitudes that agree with who you say you are. If you see yourself as a person who is honest, you will reject attitudes that rationalize cheating on exams or stealing office supplies. If you see yourself as a victim, you will always be expecting the worst to happen to you.

Attitudes Change

Does this mean that attitudes are unchanging? After all, you are who you are. You cannot change the experiences you have had or the family you were raised in. But you can, through education and maturity, change negative attitudes into positive ones.

Your attitudes change with age

Remember how, as a child, you vowed that you would be the world's most understanding parent? You would never give your child an early curfew or take the car keys away because of poor grades. But as you mature, your attitude toward those events changes. You can see that your parents were not being vindictive or old-fashioned. They were enforcing limits that were in your best interests. As a parent, your attitude may have changed so much that you will do the same things your parents did.

Your attitudes can also change with education

Prejudice is a learned attitude that leads to discrimination and stereotyping of people of different racial and ethnic backgrounds. Through education, you can overcome prejudicial attitudes and learn to see each person as unique.

Attitudes Differ

Today's workforce is made up of a diverse mix of people. In your career, you will find yourself working with people of both sexes, and from different races, cultures, ethnic and religious backgrounds. You will work with people of all ages and sizes, from many socioeconomic backgrounds, with different sexual orientations and widely different experiences and opinions. Human relations is essential in today's work environment to allow different people to cooperate and work together productively. Your attitude can make good communication on the job easy, or it can make it impossible.

Differences Are Good

People do not need to have the same attitudes to work together well or to do a competent job. There is plenty of room for differences of opinion. In fact, diversity can be good.

Jane and Doris have different approaches to childcare. The different types of family daycare they provide give parents a choice of where to send their children. They are both good childcare providers, and the satisfied parents and happy children in their care prove this. Although their attitudes toward daycare differ, they like their jobs and care deeply about the children. They approach their business with positive attitudes.

Many supervisors are skilled in reading the attitudes of their employees. You show your attitude in many ways:

in your approach to a job,

in your willingness to follow directions,

in the way you handle problems,

in your reaction to criticism, and

in the way you relate to co-workers.

A positive attitude will have a positive impact on your career. If you are energetic, motivated, productive, alert, and friendly, your co-workers will respond positively to you.

Attitudes Are Contagious

Attitudes are easily spread through a group of workers, and a positive attitude will make your work environment a pleasant place to be.

A positive attitude will also be transmitted to customers. A worker with a negative attitude will drain energy from the group. Co-workers and customers will avoid him or her, and the supervisor will see him as a less valuable employee.

In the chapters to come, you will learn ways to recognize negative attitudes and tips to help you change negative attitudes and behaviors to positive ones.

Review

Consider the answers you gave before reading the concepts. If you feel that you understood the situation and are satisfied with your first answer, write "no change" on the line. If you feel you have new insights or understanding, write your new answer or additional information.

How would you characterize Jane's attitude toward her job? How would you characterize Doris's attitude?

_____

_____

Is Jane a better daycare provider than Doris? Is Doris a better provider than Jane? Or are they equally competent?

_____

_____

How did Doris's attitude toward the classes affect what she learned? How did it affect the class?

_____

_____

How did Jane's attitude toward the classes affect what she learned? How did it affect the class?

_____

_____

Discussion

1. In your own words, define attitude.

_____

_____

_____

2. Look inward and try to identify one of your attitudes that affected your human relations at work and at school.

_____

_____

_____

Productivity and Human Relations

Case Study 3
Productivity and Human Relations

After completing this chapter, you will:

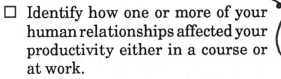

- ☐ Recognize the importance of productivity in the workplace.

- ☐ Identify how one or more of your human relationships affected your productivity either in a course or at work.

- ☐ Explain the role of human relations and attitude in productivity.

Dan Reynolds was both excited and nervous as he reported for work his first day at Shop & Save. Although he had delivered newspapers for years and had steady customers for whom he mowed lawns and shoveled snow, this was his first job in the real working world. Dan was 18, looking forward to college in six months. He needed a steady job to save money. Dan had applied for the job of stockboy at the supermarket. He was hired and would be working two hours a day after school and all day Saturday.

Dan caught on quickly to what he was supposed to do. The work was not complicated, but it did require Dan to organize his time. Each stockboy had a specific area to keep stocked. Dan was assigned to the frozen food department, with Carl and Andy, two boys he knew slightly from school.

Dan liked his job. He was a conscientious kid, punching in on time and doing his assigned work quickly and efficiently. Dan was no drudge, though. He was friendly and outgoing. He liked people and they responded to that. One of the things he liked best about his job was getting to know

all the other people in the stockroom in h
was well-liked, both by the other boys and

Dan noticed that the other stockboys
spend up to half an hour hanging aroun
beginning an assignment. Some took freq
always greeted his co-workers pleasantly, and spent a few
minutes catching up on grades and sports and the latest
news. Then he went right to work.

It was natural that some areas needed more or less
stocking on different days. Carl and Andy did not seem to
mind when the work was unfinished at the end of their shift.
But it bothered Dan to see empty shelves. He knew how
important it was to the shoppers and the store managers to
have well-stocked grocery shelves. Some days he would stay
an extra 10 or 15 minutes to complete his assigned tasks.

Dan felt uncomfortable when he was idle. Rather than
waiting around between assignments or when he was done
early, he began helping Carl and Andy finish their tasks.
Carl and Andy were grateful for the extra help. But at the
same time, they felt a little funny about Dan helping them
out. They liked him a lot—he was almost always cheerful,
and even when he'd had a bad day at school, he did not let
it affect his attitude at work. They realized that they were
making extra work for Dan when they spent time talking or
did not do their best. They did not discuss this, but both of
them began giving a little extra effort. There were even days
when they were done early enough to help Dan.

Their supervisor noticed that the frozen food section was
consistently the most well-stocked part of the store. He let
the boys know how pleased he was with their productivity.
They each were given excellent reviews and a 25-cent an
hour raise. Newly hired stockboys were sent to train with
them before being given permanent assignments. After
three months, Dan, Carl, and Andy were promoted, becoming head stockboys in three separate areas of the store.

How would you characterize Dan's attitude toward his job?

_____

_____

How did Dan's arrival at Shop & Save affect the productivity of the stockboys?

_____

_____

Can you predict another outcome if Dan had worked to increase only his own productivity?

_____

_____

Concepts

Every business must make a profit to remain in business. A car manufacturer needs to produce quality cars at a competitive price. A grocery store needs to produce sales to cover its cost of doing business and to make a profit. A police department must produce a safer city, with fewer crimes and more criminal cases solved, to please taxpayers.

Productivity and Profit

Productivity is the ability to produce the greatest amount of goods and services at the lowest possible cost. Increasing productivity will increase a company's profits.

Happy People Work Harder

The goal of good human relations is to produce happy people. The goal of good human relations in the workplace is to produce happy employees *who work hard to produce more.* Productivity is the goal of almost all group activity in our society.

Valued workers, like Dan, keep their personal productivity high. High producers also contribute to the productivity of other workers, both by completing their tasks and by serving as an example to other workers. Dan may be young, but he is good at combining human relations and productivity. Dan's attitude toward work makes him a valued employee. He approaches his job in such a way that his personal productivity is very high. And he manages to do this without alienating the other stockboys—a tribute to his good human relations skills.

The Team Player

Dan could have approached his job differently. He could have adopted the attitude that he was better than the other boys. Instead of helping Carl and Andy with their tasks, he could have pointed out to his supervisor how well-stocked his own area was. Dan's personal productivity would have been high, but the productivity of his group would not have increased. Carl and Andy would probably have grown to resent Dan. Their productivity might even have decreased as a result of their resentment. The frozen food department would not have been a pleasant place to work!

Dan is practicing two important human relations skills related to productivity. They are:

1. Increase your personal productivity by doing the best job that you can.

2. Increase group productivity by looking for ways to help your co-workers increase productivity.

Cooperation among a group of employees results in increased productivity for several reasons. When information is pooled, the group gains insight into problems. Sharing information leads to problem-solving and fewer errors.

Every Individual Is Unique

Because each of us is unique, everyone has a different potential. Even if you always work to capacity, your personal productivity potential will be different from that of your co-workers'. One worker on an assembly line may be able to assemble 200 items a day. Another worker may have the potential for completing only 175. Both are valued contributors when they work to reach their full potential.

Unique people possess unique attitudes and skills. Different people also have different attitudes, skills, and talents. Some workers may have exceptional writing skills, others may be outstanding with facts and figures. Cooperation between co-workers who share their skills and talents for the good of the group will lead to increased group productivity.

Review

Consider the answers you gave before reading the concepts. If you feel that you understood the situation and are satisfied with your first answer, write "no change" on the line. If you feel you have new insights or understanding, write your new answer or additional information.

How would you characterize Dan's attitude toward his job?

_____

_____

How did Dan's arrival at Shop & Save affect the productivity of the stockboys?

_____

_____

Identify an outcome if Dan had worked to increase only his own productivity?

_____

_____

Identify an outcome that you achieved because you worked to increase your own productivity.

_____

_____

Discussion

1. Identify an incident, either your own or a friend's, when recognizing an individual's uniqueness resulted in increased productivity.

_____

_____

_____

2. Why are human relations skills important to productivity?

_____

_____

_____

HORIZONTAL RELATIONSHIPS

Case Study 4
Horizontal Relationships

After completing this chapter, you will:

- ☐ Define horizontal relationships.

- ☐ Recognize the importance of good horizontal relationships in the workplace.

- ☐ Identify the importance of attitude in horizontal relationships.

E ileen, Kevin, and June work in the public relations department of a large metropolitan hospital. Because of their different personalities, and because their department is small and they must work closely together, they have had some disagreements.

Eileen is the creative force. She has been with Western Hospital three years and is the senior member of the department. In addition to developing new promotions, Eileen arranges the educational programs at the hospital. Her bubbly personality and openness attract people. Kevin and June like her and look to her when they have problems.

Kevin has been with the hospital a little more than a year. In that time, his job responsibilities changed. Kevin was hired to handle media relations, writing press releases, making public statements, and editing the employee newsletter. Will, the department manager, soon realized that Kevin was not a strong writer.

Kevin was valuable to the public relations department because he enjoyed being in public, attending hospital fairs, and talking to reporters. He also understood the office computer system. Will changed Kevin's job description.

Kevin would handle the clerical and computer work. He would also continue to represent the hospital at fairs and on the local radio and television newscasts.

Will hired June to do the writing. Kevin was not pleased. He felt that his writing skills were adequate and resented what he saw as a demotion. He was realistic enough to realize that a sullen attitude would be unprofessional, however, and did his best to hide his feelings. Eileen, aware of Kevin's dissatisfaction, tried to boost his ego by complimenting him when he completed projects on time.

June was aware that there would be some hard feelings over her joining the department. Her first few days, Kevin was representing the hospital at a conference. June was secretly relieved over this. Eileen and June, those first few days, found that they worked well together.

There was a noticeable chill in the air when Kevin returned. June did not feel that it was her responsibility to make the first move. And Kevin could not see why he should go out of his way to be friends with June. After a week, no one in the office was happy. Eileen continued to offer support and encouragement to both June and Kevin. She knew this was their problem to work out and did all she could to avoid the appearance of siding with one or the other.

June decided to make the first move. She did sympathize with Kevin. She could imagine how hard it must be to have someone else doing a job that was once yours. June invited Kevin to lunch and told him how she felt. Kevin was surprised to hear June talk so openly about her feelings, but he was also relieved to have the chance to clear the air.

June knew that Kevin was proud of his computer skills. She asked him to help her learn the system. She also asked him for his ideas about the newsletter. She told him that she was counting on him to show her the ropes. Kevin responded positively to June's overtures. He was also unhappy about the tension.

Your Analysis

How would you characterize Eileen's attitude toward her job and co-workers? June's attitude? Kevin's attitude?

_____

_____

How would you describe the early horizontal relationships in the public relations department?

_____

_____

How would you describe their horizontal relationships after one month?

_____

_____

Can you imagine a different outcome for this case study? Would your outcome increase or decrease productivity?

_____

_____

Concepts

Anytime two people have contact on a frequent basis, a relationship exists between them. It may be a good relationship; it may be not so good; sometimes it may even be bad or destructive. But rarely will a relationship be neutral.

In your social life, you can choose those you wish to have a relationship with. In your working life, however, you have no choice. You will have a relationship with your co-workers, and it is in the best interests of your career and the productivity of your company that these relationships be positive ones.

What Is a Good Relationship?

What does a good working relationship involve? It does not mean that the people you work with need to become your best friends. It does mean that you interact with one another in such a way that your personal goals and company goals are achieved. These relationships with co-workers are called horizontal relationships.

Every relationship is different, because every person sees you, your personality, and your attitude differently. How you view another person is influenced by your personal prejudices, likes, and dislikes. How others view you is affected in the same way. As a result, good relationships are built differently with different people.

Horizontal Relationships

Eileen and June developed a good *horizontal relationship* rather quickly because they had no preconceived notions about each other. It was harder for Kevin and June to establish a good relationship. Kevin felt June was an intruder who had taken part of his job away. He saw her as a threat to his job security and also as a reminder that he was not a good writer. This was a major block in the development of a good horizontal relationship between them.

The most important element in developing good horizontal relationships with your co-workers is free and open communication. Good communication allows the exchange of ideas and suggestions. Minor complaints and problems can be discussed and resolved before they become major ones. June knew this. She was aware that doing a good job would be very hard without Kevin's cooperation.

Your Responsibility

By inviting Kevin to lunch, June was demonstrating another important point. The primary responsibility for establishing horizontal relationships is yours. You cannot wait for the other person to make the first move. June has helped resolve a situation that could have dragged on for months, causing tension and reducing productivity.

Kevin contributed to the development of a good relationship by being open to June's overtures. Rather than nurse a grudge, he agreed to share his experience and knowledge.

Eileen has also contributed to the solution by remaining impartial. She has maintained her good relationships with both Kevin and June by encouraging their efforts but letting them resolve their differences by themselves.

By the end of their first month together, June, Eileen, and Kevin were functioning as a team. Although they are very different from each other, they have built a productive department. Their skills and talents complement one another and contribute to the productivity of their group.

Vertical Relationships

Establishing good horizontal relationships will also enhance your vertical relationship with your supervisor. Will noticed the tension between June and Kevin. He also noticed when their relationship improved. He appreciated their professionalism in working out their differences by themselves. They have helped their careers by their efforts to communicate.

You can see how important it is to have a good horizontal relationship between people who work together closely. It is also good to develop relationships with others in your company. Often, departments must work together, on a day-to-day-basis or an occasional special project. Make an effort to know the others in your organization.

Human Relations and Networking

It is a good idea to develop good horizontal relationships with people outside your company whom you contact in the course of business. Establishing contacts with people who can help you in your career is known as networking.

Review

Consider the answers you gave before reading the concepts. If you feel that you understood the situation and are satisfied with your first answer, write "no change" on the line. If you feel you have new insights or understanding, write your new answer or additional information.

How would you characterize Eileen's attitude toward her job and co-workers? June's attitude? Kevin's attitude?

_____

_____

How would you describe the early horizontal relationships in the public relations department?

_____

_____

How would you describe their horizontal relationships after one month?

_____

_____

Can you imagine a different outcome for this case study? Would your outcome increase or decrease productivity?

_____

_____

Discussion

1. Identify one of your horizontal relationships.

   _____

   _____

   _____

2. Identify how a horizontal relationship, either at school or work, improved your networking ability.

   _____

   _____

   _____

3. What role did your attitude play in the development of this good horizontal relationship?

   _____

   _____

   _____

VERTICAL RELATIONSHIPS

Case Study 5
Vertical Relationships

After completing this chapter, you will:

☐ Define vertical relationships.

☐ Recognize how good vertical and horizontal relationships interact.

☐ Identify the importance of a good attitude in establishing both good vertical and horizontal relationships.

George Skinta supervises the accounting department in a large manufacturing firm. After 14 years on the job, he was an experienced manager. He had worked his way up from accounting assistant to supervisor. Because of this, he thought of himself as a competent supervisor who understood the problems faced by his employees. For the most part, the people under his supervision seemed happy. He was proud of their accuracy and high productivity rate.

The workers in the accounting department saw George as a fair and honest boss. They appreciated that he did not play favorites. They all knew that they could go to George with a problem and he would do his best to solve it. They had good horizontal relationships with one another and were happy in their jobs.

Recently, a new employee had been hired. Mike Patterson was fresh out of school, anxious to make good. Mike knew he had the skills to succeed in the position, and the people seemed nice. He and George seemed to hit it off.

Mike made a good impression on his co-workers. He was young and eager, quick to ask questions, and thankful for advice from the older workers. They could see he knew his business and would definitely be an asset to the department.

George liked Mike. He was reminded of himself 20 years ago. One night, after working late on a project, George and Mike went to dinner. They discovered how much they had in common. Mike had even grown up in George's old neighborhood. Mike asked George's advice about his career, and George was pleased to be in the position of mentor to a young man with so much on the ball.

George and Mike began spending more time together off the job. Without being aware of it, George was giving Mike a little extra attention on the job also. Mike's co-workers noticed the growing friendship between Mike and their boss. When a particularly desirable assignment came up, George gave it to Mike. He had valid reasons for doing so. It was an excellent learning experience for a new worker and was in the field that Mike had majored in. But Mike's co-workers saw it differently. They were sure that George had assigned Mike to the job because of their growing friendship.

The uneasiness of the other employees began affecting their relationship with Mike. They began to see him as a threat to their careers. They were short with him when he came to them for advice. They stopped asking him to lunch with them. Mike felt excluded and could not figure out why. He had no idea what he had done to upset his fellow workers.

Their unhappiness interfered with their previously excellent relationship with George. They no longer saw him as fair and impartial. They felt that he was favoring Mike. They began putting less energy into their work, and productivity in the accounting department declined.

George heard the grumblings. He knew that Mike was having a hard time making friends. He also was displeased with the decline in productivity. He had thought everything was going along so well. What was wrong?

Your Analysis

How would you characterize the vertical relationship between George and his staff before Mike was hired? After Mike was hired?

_____

_____

Do you think there is a problem in the vertical relationship between Mike and George?

_____

_____

What can Mike do to improve his horizontal relationships?

_____

_____

What can George do to improve his relationship with his staff?

_____

_____

Concepts

A vertical relationship is the relationship between you and your supervisor. Developing a strong vertical relationship can be essential to your progress on the job. The development of good vertical relationships has much in common with the development of good horizontal relationships. Both depend on effective communication between two people. But there are some important differences.

Supervisor's Responsibility

The primary responsibility for creating a good vertical relationship lies not with you, but with your supervisor. He or she will set the tone for interactions between boss and employee. Realizing this, many businesses provide their managers and supervisors with training in interpersonal relationships. However, you must do your share to establish a strong vertical relationship with your supervisor. Like all relationships between two people, it is a two-way street.

Some offices are casual—everyone, including supervisors, is on a first-name basis. There may be loose job descriptions, with many crossovers in job responsibilities. Other offices will be more traditional. You will be expected to refer to your supervisor by Mr. or Mrs. They may address you the same way. Job descriptions may be more rigid and employee interactions more formal.

The tone of your office may be influenced by the type of business conducted. The personality of the department manager will be a contributing factor, also. Neither type of office is better, but different people may work more effectively in one than in the other.

You need to recognize what type of supervisor you have and what kind of office environment you are working in. Verbal and nonverbal office communication will give you clues. The way other employees address the supervisor and one another is one important clue.

Vertical Dangers

An overly strong vertical relationship can weaken horizontal relationships. Mike's good relationship with his co-workers deteriorated as his vertical relationship with George became stronger. A particular friendship between a supervisor and one or two employees can create jealousy and threaten other workers. It can adversely affect the morale and productivity of a department. It is important that a manager avoid favoritism and even the appearance of favoritism.

The good relationships George had developed over the years with the people under his supervision were endangered because they feared that his friendship with Mike threatened their job security and chance for advancement. George needs to strengthen his vertical relationships with the others as well as with Mike. He must let them know that he is not favoring Mike.

Mike needs to spend extra time on his horizontal relationships. He needs to let his co-workers know that he is a hardworking and productive member of the department and that he is not benefiting unfairly from his relationship with George. Mike is discovering the benefits and drawbacks to developing a mentor relationship with a supervisor.

As you work on developing a good vertical relationship, do not neglect your horizontal relationships. Your success in your career and the productivity of your department depend on both types of relationships being strong.

Review

Consider the answers you gave before reading the concepts. If you feel that you understood the situation and are satisfied with your first answer, write "no change" on the line. If you feel you have new insights or understanding, write your new answer or additional information.

How would you characterize the vertical relationship between George and his staff before Mike was hired? After Mike was hired?

_____

_____

Do you think there is a problem in the vertical relationship between Mike and George?

_____

_____

What can Mike do to improve his horizontal relationships?

_____

_____

What can George do to improve his relationship with his staff?

_____

_____

Discussion

1. Identify one of your vertical relationships.

_____

_____

_____

2. Identify how a good vertical relationship (at school or work) improved your horizontal relationship.

_____

_____

_____

3. What role did your attitude play in the development of this good vertical relationship?

_____

_____

_____

DESTRUCTIVE ATTITUDES

6

Case Study 6
Destructive Attitudes

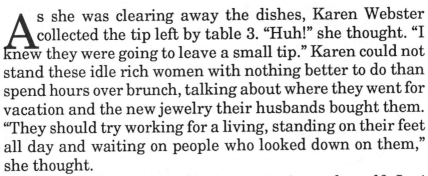

After completing this chapter, you will:

- ☐ Define and identify destructive attitudes.

- ☐ Recognize the negative effect of destructive attitudes on the job.

- ☐ Identify a destructive attitude in either you or a friend that had a negative effect on the job or in a class.

As she was clearing away the dishes, Karen Webster collected the tip left by table 3. "Huh!" she thought. "I knew they were going to leave a small tip." Karen could not stand these idle rich women with nothing better to do than spend hours over brunch, talking about where they went for vacation and the new jewelry their husbands bought them. "They should try working for a living, standing on their feet all day and waiting on people who looked down on them," she thought.

Karen went into the kitchen muttering to herself. José asked her what the problem was, but she gave him a look that clearly said, "Don't bother me." José shook his head. Karen had not forgiven him for the mistake he made last week, when he mixed up her order with Susan's. He had overheard her telling Susan: "That José doesn't even try to improve his English. I can't stand these people who come here and think they're too good to learn our language." It still upset him to think about it. He was glad Susan had defended him, telling Karen it was an easy mistake to make.

The lunchtime crowd was slow. Lately, business had been dropping off because of that new restaurant downtown. As Karen waited on her tables, she could hear Susan's laughter from across the room. "Honestly," she thought, "you'd think she was having a good time instead of working."

Karen just wanted to get people in and out as soon as possible. That was the sign of an efficient waitress, she believed, not whether or not your customers liked you. Oh, sure, it was worth giving a little extra personal service to the businessmen. They had the money to tip well.

Why did Susan bother wasting her time making polite conversation with those welfare bums? They were not going to leave a big tip. And those people from the senior citizens' complex—if they were too broke to tip, they should just stay home. Most of them were half-blind or deaf, and you had to keep repeating the menu to them. "Good thing they don't sit on my side of the room anymore," Karen decided.

At the end of her shift that day, Norman, the restaurant manager, called her into his office. As soon as the door closed, Karen began a litany of complaints. "When Susan lets customers linger over their coffee, I end up with more people at my station. It's not fair. And José is too dense to learn English. And..."

"That's enough, Karen." Norman stopped her in mid-sentence. "It's obvious that you are just not cut out to be in the service business. As you know, business is off. I have to let one waitress go. I'm afraid it's you."

"What are you talking about?" Karen was stunned. "I'm the most efficient waitress you have! I never make mistakes—at least not ones that are my fault—and I get people in and out quickly. Susan is not as efficient as I am."

Norman nodded. "That's true, Karen. You are efficient. But your attitude upsets my customers. You let your personal feelings affect your service. And your prejudices are getting in the way of your performance on the job. I'm afraid my decision is final."

Destructive Attitudes

Your Analysis

How would you characterize Karen's attitude toward her job? Toward her customers?

_____

_____

How did Karen's attitude affect her job performance?

_____

_____

Did Norman make the right decision?

_____

_____

How could Karen have been a better employee?

_____

_____

Concepts

The most efficient worker in the world will find job success elusive without a good attitude. Your attitude affects your relationships with your boss and with your co-workers. Your attitude also influences your interactions with customers.

Productivity Plus Positive Attitude

Karen was an efficient waitress. However, her attitude was destructive. It adversely affected her relationships with José and with the restaurant customers. Susan may have been a slightly less efficient waitress than Karen, but her constructive attitude more than made up for it. Customers were pleased with her service. They were more likely to return. The service industry needs people who combine high productivity with a pleasant, positive attitude like Susan's.

Prejudices

Destructive attitudes have a negative impact on everything you do. Karen might be surprised to be labeled a racist, but her interactions with José are negatively affected by her attitude toward immigrants. Racism is a destructive attitude that has profoundly influenced our society. People have been denied basic human rights because of the color of their skin or their country of origin.

Ageism—discriminating against others because of their age—affects Karen's attitude toward senior citizens. Rather than seeing them as individuals deserving of her attention, she looks at her elderly customers as part of a bothersome group.

The destructive attitude of sexism influences our relationships with male and female employees, supervisors, and customers. An example of sexism is wrongly assuming a person cannot perform some jobs simply because of his or her sex.

Racism, ageism, and sexism are examples of prejudices. A prejudice is an adverse or harmful opinion based on a generalization—often incorrect—about a group of people. Prejudices are obstacles to good human relations because they prevent us from seeing each person as an individual. They cut off communication between two people.

Karen's prejudice has prevented her from seeing José as a productive member of a team. Unlike Susan, she does not see him as an individual, but as one of "those people." Not only has it interfered with her developing a friendly relationship with José, but it has interfered with her ability to work with him.

Prejudice can be responsible for destructive actions like playing favorites. It can lead to arrogance or outright rudeness in your dealing with others. You may underestimate or overestimate those you work with because of your attitude about their race, age, or sex.

Oversensitivity

Another destructive attitude that can limit your effectiveness on the job is oversensitivity—taking slights and mistakes personally. The overly sensitive worker may spend more time nursing wounded feelings than performing required tasks. Small gripes can become major upsets for people who are overly sensitive.

Selfishness

Selfish people have the attitude that their needs and concerns are more important than anyone else's. They are unable to put aside self-involvement for the good of another person or of their employer. Workers with a selfish attitude will arrive late, never giving a thought to the effect on their co-workers who had to cover for them. Because they are primarily concerned with themselves, they are often tactless and inconsiderate in their dealings with others.

Dissatisfaction

Dissatisfaction is a destructive attitude that can take the joy out of a job for yourself and those who work with you. Everyone knows at least one person who never seems satisfied. The salary is too low, the working conditions are bad, the last raise was too small, the customers are rude. One dissatisfied worker can reduce everyone else's productivity.

Nobody likes to be around a Gloomy Gus. Always looking for the negative side of people and situations can become a full-time occupation. The energy used in dwelling on the negatives can be put to better use looking for the positive.

You may not be aware of your destructive responses to people and situations, because your attitude is often an unconscious reaction on your part.

Take the time to examine your responses to co-workers, supervisors, and customers.

Analyze your reaction to situations that confront you on the job.

Ask yourself:

Are my attitudes constructive ones or destructive ones?

Do I respond to situations in a positive or a negative way?

Does my attitude help communication or hinder it?

Review

Consider the answers you gave before reading the concepts. If you feel that you understood the situation and are satisfied with your first answer, write "no change" on the line. If you feel you have new insights or understanding, write your new answer or additional information.

How would you characterize Karen's attitude toward her job? Toward her customers?

_____

_____

How did Karen's attitude affect her job performance?

_____

_____

Did Norman make the right decision?

_____

_____

How could Karen have been a better employee?

_____

_____

Discussion

1. Define destructive attitude and give examples of specific ones.

   _____

   _____

   _____

2. What impact has a destructive attitude, either yours, a peer's, or a supervisor's, had on your job or studies?

   _____

   _____

   _____

Case Study 7
Constructive Attitudes

After completing this chapter, you will:

- ☐ Define and identify constructive attitudes.

- ☐ Recognize the difference between a positive attitude and a constructive attitude.

- ☐ Identify the effect a constructive attitude has had on your job or a class.

Rose Potter and Irene Loomis were cashiers at Hammond's Department Store. They were both good workers, accurate and experienced. There was rarely any problem with their cash drawers balancing at the end of the day. They both kept informed about weekly sales and specials.

Like many other department stores in the area, Hammond's was finding it hard to find and keep good workers. They needed to compete with the salaries offered by nearby fast-food restaurants and the new shopping center across town.

Mr. Hammond believed that one way of keeping good employees was to recognize their efforts and let them know how much they were appreciated. He posted a notice on the employee bulletin board announcing an award for Employee of the Month. The winner would receive a $50 bonus check and have his or her picture displayed for a month. The announcement was well-received by the employees. Nobody would mind receiving an extra $50!

Mr. Hammond had many good employees. For the first month, he decided to honor one outstanding worker who had been with Hammond's for several years. After three weeks, he had narrowed his choice to Rose or Irene. Their work records were excellent. They arrived on time and did not abuse their sick leave. Their accuracy was commendable. They approached their work in a professional fashion that pleased him. It was a hard choice to make.

Mr. Hammond spent a little extra time observing Rose and Irene at work. It was then that he noticed something a bit odd. When it was busy, both women had long lines of customers at their cash registers. But Mr. Hammond noticed that his regular customers seldom went in Irene's line; they headed straight for Rose. In fact, when business was slow, there might be two or three regular customers waiting to check out with Rose while Irene's line would be empty.

It did not take Mr. Hammond long to figure out why this happened. Although efficient and friendly, Irene never took the time to offer suggestions or money-saving tips to her customers. If customers asked a question, Irene would smile and say that she would be happy to hold their purchases at the counter while they could go back and check on an item. Mr. Hammond was dismayed to see that Irene frequently let customers buy items that were incorrectly marked or could be bought with coupons.

Mr. Hammond also saw why Rose was a favorite of the long-time customers. She had a pleasant hello and a smile for everyone. In addition, Rose would remind customers of special sales and alternative products that cost less. Mr. Hammond was impressed that she gave her customers good advice that saved them money or offered better quality. It might take Rose an extra 30 seconds to check someone out because of this, but it was time well spent. The customers clearly appreciated Rose's personal touch.

Mr. Hammond knew who his first Employee of the Month would be.

Your Analysis

Compare and contrast Rose's attitude with Irene's.

_____

_____

Which cashier has a constructive attitude? How is this attitude communicated to customers?

_____

_____

Whom would you choose for Employee of the Month? Why?

_____

_____

Concepts

Developing and maintaining a constructive attitude can mean the difference between success and failure on the job. It can be the difference between productive relationships with your customers, co-workers, and supervisor or simply pleasant ones that hinder customer satisfaction.

A Constructive Attitude Leads to Productivity

A positive attitude alone cannot make up for a lack of human relations skills. In fact, a nice smile that takes the place of helping a customer find what he or she is looking for may even be patronizing and phoney. Although Rose and Irene are equally positive and friendly workers, Rose's knowledgeable advice and friendly attitude make her the more valuable employee.

Some people seem as if they are born with a constructive attitude. In any given situation, they look for new ways to help others solve problems. Their positive aspects make them cheerful and friendly, but people are attracted to them because they are also helpful.

Being around a person with a positive attitude makes you feel better than being around someone who is often gloomy and depressed. But a constructive attitude combines a smile with efficiency and knowledge, and this leads to productivity.

More Than Just a Smile

A constructive attitude is more than just a smile, although presenting a friendly face is important. An important element of a constructive attitude is being interested in others to the point of sincerely helping them solve problems.

This will help you at work the same way it helps Rose. Rose created good will among Hammond's customers by taking a personal interest in them. This helped them feel special and valued.

Everyone Wants to Feel Important

Everyone wants to feel that he or she is important and not just another nameless face in the crowd. Rose's constructive attitude also enhances her relationships with her co-workers and with Mr. Hammond. A willingness to help others leads to ties that bind.

Constructive Attitudes Bring Positive Responses

Constructive attitudes bring positive responses. If your attitude says, "I'm here to help you as best I can," others are more likely to approach you in a positive way. Even if you cannot help, they will remember your constructive attitude.

Getting Through Bad Days

Everyone has bad days. Worries about family, health, or money can interfere with your interactions at work. It's hard to smile at a customer or co-worker when you are worried about something. If you have a constructive attitude, these days are the exception, not the rule. Valued workers do their best to help others and by doing so, they forget their own problems.

Review

Consider the answers you gave before reading the concepts. If you feel that you understood the situation and are satisfied with your first answer, write "no change" on the line. If you feel you have new insights or understanding, write your new answer or additional information.

Compare and contrast Rose's attitude with Irene's.

_____

_____

Which cashier has a constructive attitude? How is this attitude communicated to customers?

_____

_____

Whom would you choose for Employee of the Month? Why?

_____

_____

Discussion

1. Define a constructive attitude you recently experienced and give an example.

_____

_____

_____

2. Identify one of your constructive attitudes and how it affected your work or class participation.

_____

_____

_____

MORALE AND JOB SATISFACTION

Case Study 8
Morale and Job Satisfaction

After completing this chapter, you will:

☐ Define morale.

☐ Identify the connection between morale and job satisfaction.

☐ Recognize the relationship between attitude and morale.

☐ Identify one of your relationships whereby you either did or did not experience a connection between morale and job satisfaction.

A nne was the receptionist at Water City's busiest beauty salon. While she enjoyed her job and the people she worked with, she felt ready for a change. Anne thought working in a doctor's office would be interesting. Skimming the classified ads one morning, she noticed an opening for an appointment secretary in a pediatric office. It sounded like the perfect job. She applied that same day.

The interview went well and she got the job. The work required two of Anne's top skills: organization and human relations. Anne met the other women in the office. The activity was nonstop as children came and went, some laughing, some crying.

Anne arrived at work early Monday. The office area was small and crowded. The appointment secretary's desk was crammed in the corner. Her chair jutted out into the aisle. The desk was piled with boxes of appointment cards and several appointment books.

Lori, Katherine, Winnie, and Sandra arrived together. They greeted Anne pleasantly, and Katherine, the office manager, told Sandra to train Anne. Anne was eager to attack the pile of appointment cards. She enjoyed creating order from chaos. But first she would have to learn to manage the front desk.

It was confusing. Anne was unfamiliar with many of the medical terms, but she was confident that she would catch on quickly. She enjoyed greeting the parents and seeing the tiny patients. But the office was so busy there was only time for a quick hello and a "sign this form, please" before the next patient arrived. The biggest problem was reading the doctors' handwriting. She kept having to ask for help.

The office had no coffee machine. When Anne asked about this, she was told that no one wanted to bother to make it. Instead, they went to the corner store for coffee. When it was break time, Anne was busy. No one asked her if she would like a coffee, and she was unaware that Lori had gone to get coffee for the others until she returned. Anne discovered quickly that she had to look out for herself.

Tuesday, Sandra was off, so Winnie trained her. Dr. Eden was the only doctor in the office. Anne liked Dr. Eden, although she soon sensed the others did not. She had an easier time reading his writing and she found him pleasant. Yesterday, Dr. Brown had not even said hello.

As time went on, Anne began to feel that she had no status. She spent most of the day on the phone, with little interaction with co-workers. She had little feedback on her performance. The doctors seemed in a different world. Katherine was often out on business. The others seemed to comment only if Anne made a mistake. Also, they gossiped about whoever was absent. Anne wondered if they talked about her when she was off.

After two months, Anne learned that her former job at the beauty salon was available. Anne gave Katherine two weeks' notice.

Your Analysis

How would you characterize Anne's morale after a day on the job? After two months?

_____

_____

How would you characterize the group morale in the pediatric office?

_____

_____

Evaluate Anne's attitude and the attitude of the others in the office. Do their attitudes affect office morale?

_____

_____

Do you agree with Anne's solution to her problem? Why or why not?

_____

_____

Concepts

Attitudes and Morale

Your attitude and the attitude of your co-workers and supervisors have a direct influence on your morale. Morale refers to your frame of mind and outlook about your job. It includes your feelings about your job, your work environment, your co-workers, and your supervisors.

A workplace where morale is high is a pleasant place to work. Customers can tell if the morale of a business is high in their interactions with the employees. When morale is high, job satisfaction is high.

Do you have a job where you look forward to going to work? Chances are you find the job interesting, challenging, or worthwhile, your relationships with your co-workers and supervisor are constructive ones, and you are working in a pleasant environment. Your morale is high.

Morale and Productivity

High group morale is one factor in increased productivity. Studies have shown that when the morale of the individual members of a group is high, absenteeism and the turnover rate are low. This increases group productivity.

Low morale can negatively affect job performance. If you are unhappy with your job responsibilities or your working environment, your attitude toward your job will be affected. Low group morale increases the rate of absenteeism and job turnover.

If you work with co-workers whose attitudes are destructive, you may find it hard to keep a positive attitude yourself. Low employee morale is often expressed by unfriendliness, annoyance, or rudeness to co-workers and customers. Workers may develop a negative attitude as the result of low morale. Sometimes, the destructive attitudes of several workers are the cause of low group morale.

Working Environment and Morale

Anne began her job with good morale and high expectations. Because her other work experience was positive, she expected to enjoy her new job. Several factors contributed to her declining morale as time went on.

One of these factors was the poorly set up work space. Crowded and cramped, the space was small and poorly organized.

The lack of effective training procedures was another factor. It was hard for Anne to feel competent and in control when she lacked information.

The attitude of her co-workers was an important factor in Anne's low morale level. Destructive behavior on their part, such as excluding Anne from their group, certainly did not make her look forward to coming to work each day.

Morale Cycles and Job Satisfaction

It is common to experience changes in your morale level over the course of your working life. Sometimes, different jobs will lead to different levels of job satisfaction. At other times, you may find yourself experiencing a cycle from high morale to low morale and back again in a job you have held for years.

As your goals change, your satisfaction level with your job may change. Anne may have decided to leave the job she enjoyed at the beauty salon because she wanted to learn new skills and face new challenges.

Confidence Levels and Morale

Changes in your level of confidence can also have an effect on your morale. As you gain knowledge and experience, your confidence and morale may be high. If you are given a job to do that you fear is beyond your capabilities, both your confidence level and your morale may fall. Once you prove to yourself that you are capable of handling the new responsibilities, your morale will rise again.

Look for Causes

If you find that you are experiencing long periods of low morale, you need to discover why. Are you doing what you want to do? Anne enjoyed working with people. One reason for her unhappiness and low morale was that her contacts with patients in the office were so limited. She missed being able to chat with her customers and co-workers as she did in the beauty salon.

Are you overqualified for your job?

Perhaps your education or experience qualify you for a more challenging position. You may miss the opportunity to expand your skills if your job requires you to do the same task day after day. Once you have mastered those tasks, you may need to find new challenges.

Are your expectations too high?

You may feel that you are not progressing fast enough. You may have expected to receive a promotion or raise that did not materialize. It might help to reevaluate your expectations and see if they are realistic.

Anne expected to feel as comfortable and welcome at her new job as at the beauty salon. This was unrealistic. All transitions take time. She may also have expected that she would have more say about organizing her area of responsibility.

This is a more realistic expectation. If Anne had remained at the doctor's office, she might have eventually been able to implement her ideas.

Talk to Your Supervisor

If you are struggling with low morale, talk to your supervisor. Describe your problem and see if he or she can offer any help. Do not focus on a laundry list of complaints or personal attacks on your co-workers. Keep the focus of the conversation on your attitude toward the job.

If the problem is low group morale, your supervisor may already be aware of it and grateful for the chance to find solutions to the problem. If Anne had discussed her unhappiness with Katherine or one of the doctors, they might have helped her find a solution to her problems. Finding a new job should be your last resort, not your first.

Review

Consider the answers you gave before reading the concepts. If you feel that you understood the situation and are satisfied with your first answer, write "no change" on the line. If you feel you have new insights or understanding, write your new answer or additional information.

How would you characterize Anne's morale after a day on the job? After two months?

_____

_____

How would you characterize the group morale in the pediatric office?

_____

_____

Evaluate Anne's attitude and the attitude of the others in the office. Do their attitudes affect morale?

_____

_____

Do you agree with Anne's solution to her problem? Why or why not?

_____

_____

Discussion

1. Can you remember when, either in a class or on a job, your morale has been very low?

_____

_____

_____

2. How did low morale affect your course or job satisfaction?

_____

_____

_____

3. Identify a friend who had low morale, and try to determine what attitude that friend had that may have affected his or her morale.

_____

_____

Handling Frustration on the Job

Case Study 9

Handling Frustration on the Job

After completing this chapter, you will:

- ☐ Identify the relationship between frustration and aggression.

- ☐ Recognize the role of attitude in minimizing frustration.

- ☐ Recognize ways in which you dealt with frustration, either positively or negatively.

Al Roman had worked for Bayshore's public works department four years. He had started right out of high school, digging ditches and repairing potholes. It was a good, secure job, perfect for an 18-year-old who was not quite sure what he wanted to do.

Al was a hard worker. Bayshore's public works department was often criticized by the local newspaper for inefficiency and poor work. Secretly Al agreed. Too many workers loafed on the job, taking long breaks, and even leaving the job site when the supervisor was away. Al could not do that.

Supervisors noticed Al's attitude. Through the years, they gave him more responsibility. When a worker was needed for a job that would have minimal supervision, Al was asked to do it; his boss knew that Al would do a good job even when not directly supervised.

Al felt one of the department's biggest problems was the Director of Public Works for Bayshore, James Martin. He had held his position for years through political influence, not competence. He gave his workers little respect and they responded in kind. He handpicked department heads—usually personal friends, often relatives. The good workers were frustrated by the inefficiency and poor management.

Luckily, Al had little contact with Mr. Martin. His immediate supervisor, John Passero, was a pleasure to work for. John let Al know how pleased he was with his work. He gave Al opportunities to prove himself. John saw that not only was Al a good worker, but when he was on the job, the others worked more steadily. John made Al chargeman because of his ability to motivate the others. He let Al know he had a good future in the department.

Al decided to take advantage of the free tuition offered by the city. He began going to night school at the local technical college.

Al was optimistic about the future, until John suffered a heart attack and could not return to work. James Martin assigned his nephew, Paul Martin, to supervise Al's crew. Al and his co-workers were stunned. Paul Martin was only 22; he had been with the department less than three years and was a poor worker.

Paul had no idea how to supervise the men. He spent most of the day in his uncle's downtown office. That was fine with the crew. The less they saw of Paul, the better. Al was still chargeman; at least that had not changed. But he no longer got any feedback. He missed John's advice and encouragement. Because no one was handling problems, small problems were becoming larger. It was getting harder to do a good job. Al buried his frustrations in an attempt to keep his relationship with Paul Martin cordial.

When the head chargeman retired, Al expected to receive the promotion. Instead, Paul Martin gave the job to his buddy, who had been on the job less than a year. Al's frustration, kept barely under control for too long, exploded. He headed downtown to confront Paul Martin. All the anger Al had kept bottled up inside spilled out. He told Paul exactly what he thought of him and of his uncle.

Your Analysis

How would you characterize Al's attitude toward
his job before Paul Martin arrived? After Paul
Martin arrived?

_____

_____

Was Al justified in his anger at Paul and James
Martin?

_____

_____

Can you think of other ways that Al could have
dealt with his frustration?

_____

_____

Concepts

You experience frustration when you are prevented from reaching a goal or fulfilling a desire. When you are late for an appointment and get stuck in traffic, or when you are expecting company for dinner and cannot find your favorite recipe, you are frustrated. There are ways to minimize frustrations—you could have left earlier for your appointment or filed your recipe away correctly after you used it. However, there is no way to avoid all frustration. Unfortunately, frustration is an inevitable part of life.

Frustration and Your Attitude

Frustration at work may be the *cause* of a destructive attitude or it may be the *result* of it. Al's attitude toward his job was constructive. His career was progressing well. His frustration grew from the changes caused by John's departure and Paul's arrival. His frustration was the ***cause*** of his destructive attitude.

If you approach your job with destructive attitudes, you will limit your opportunity for advancement. This can lead to frustration because you do not reach the goal you have set for yourself. In this case, frustration is the ***result*** of a destructive attitude. Developing constructive attitudes will help you eliminate this type of frustration.

Dealing With Frustration

Frustrations do not just go away. They need to be dealt with, one way or another. If you do not find a way of addressing the frustrations you experience every day, they will build up, affecting your performance and attitude.

How you deal with frustration on the job can affect your career positively or negatively. Even in a job you love, you will experience frustration at some point. There are acceptable and unacceptable ways to deal with this.

Unacceptable Reactions

Anger and aggression are unacceptable ways of relieving frustration. In a job situation, they can damage your career and your relationships with others.

Al let his frustration build to the point where his anger exploded. He has damaged his relationship with his supervisor and also with the director of public works. He may find that he is fired or that, in his anger, he quits his job. He will lose what he has worked for, his educational benefits, and any chance he may have had for future promotions. He has lost the opportunity to bring his grievance to a third party and have it resolved. Verbal aggression can have far-reaching and unwanted consequences.

Another unacceptable way of dealing with frustration is sabotaging company goals by your performance. Work slowdowns or work stoppages may make you feel temporarily better. They serve no constructive purpose, however. The cause of your frustration is still there, and your poor performance will bring negative consequences sooner or later. Your work slowdowns will often cause your co-workers to pick up the slack, and they will resent this.

Acceptable Reactions

It is a good idea to **seek** the advice of a third party when you are experiencing frustration with someone or something on the job. But choose your confidant wisely. Avoid downgrading co-workers and your company. Words spoken in anger or to the wrong person can come back to haunt you. Talking with someone you trust about your frustrations can give you insights into how to handle them.

Maintaining a constructive attitude will be easier if you have an outlet for your aggression. **Physical** activity is an excellent way to discharge negative energy. When you feel your frustration level rising, try to release it in an acceptable way.

Walk, run, bicycle, swim, play handball; clean closets, scrub floors, weed the garden.

At work, do something physical if you possibly can, like reorganizing a messy storage room, scrubbing the office coffee pot, or using your break to take a brisk walk.

Slamming doors and desk drawers will not improve your standing in the eyes of your co-workers or your supervisor.

Put your frustrations into writing

Many people find that keeping a journal helps them to release frustration and even solve problems. Putting your feelings down on paper can help you to analyze them. You may discover why you are feeling frustrated.

Never write and send a letter or memo in anger

Angry spoken words may eventually be forgotten. Angry written words will be around long after the frustration that prompted them is gone.

Keep It in Perspective

Sometimes, you may find yourself on the receiving end of aggressive feelings from supervisors, co-workers, or customers. Your supervisor may be frustrated after reading the latest sales figures. If you are the next person to walk into the room, you may find that anger and frustration directed at you. In most cases, you, personally, are not the cause of the frustration. Remembering this can help you avoid overreacting in ways that damage your relationships.

Dealing with frustration at work is easier if you can keep it in perspective. Work is a major part of your life and your identity, but it should not be the only thing. Family, friends, and hobbies are important in helping you deal with the stress you encounter every day.

If work is all you do and all you have, then the frustration you encounter at work may become all-consuming.

Developing relationships outside of work will help you deal with job frustration.

Spending your time away from work with people whose company you enjoy, and doing activities you like, will help you approach your job with a positive attitude.

Review

Consider the answers you gave before reading the concepts. If you feel that you understood the situation and are satisfied with your first answer, write "no change" on the line. If you feel you have new insights or understanding, write your new answer or additional information.

How would you characterize Al's attitude toward his job before Paul Martin arrived? After Paul Martin arrived?

_____

_____

Was Al justified in his anger at Paul and James Martin?

_____

_____

Can you think of other ways that Al could have dealt with his frustration?

_____

_____

Discussion

1. What is the relationship between frustration and aggression?

_____

_____

_____

2. How does your attitude affect the way you handle frustration?

_____

_____

_____

3. List several ways in which you have dealt with frustration either on your job or at school.

_____

_____

_____

THE RUMOR MILL

Case Study 10
The Rumor Mill

WHISPER

WHISPER

After completing this chapter, you will:

- ☐ Identify the negative impact of rumors on the job.

- ☐ Recognize the role of attitude in the development and passing of rumors.

- ☐ Identify a time when it would have been wiser for you to maintain a constructive attitude and avoid participating in the rumor mill.

Last week, Maria Minton had been asked to handle a problem: the late delivery of an important shipment. The customer, one of Peterson Paper's largest accounts, was irate and threatened to find a new supplier.

Maria was surprised to be given such an important assignment, because she was fairly new. It was exciting to face such a challenge. She used all her customer relations skills to come up with a solution that satisfied the customer and pleased her supervisor, Lee Davids.

"Maria," Lee said, "You did a wonderful job with that problem shipment. I've been watching your work, and I had no doubt that you could handle it. I told Mr. Peterson that you saved the account. There'll be a bonus in your paycheck. If you keep up the good work, I expect that within six months you'll be in charge of our customer relations department."

Maria could hardly believe her ears. When her co-worker Judith invited her to lunch, Maria eagerly accepted. "Wait until I tell you my good news!" Maria said.

"I'm happy for you, Maria," Judith said at lunch. "But don't get your hopes up about that promotion. Lee's buddy, Bill, told me he was sure he'd get that job. Everyone knows he's next in line. If you'd been here longer, you'd know that Lee often makes promises he doesn't keep."

Maria was deflated. Still, she resolved to do her best. As the months went on, she was given more important accounts. Several times, Lee praised her performance.

Maria's only regret was that friendships she had formed at the office were faltering. Judith occasionally asked her to lunch, but Maria felt uncomfortable accepting. Lately, her lunches with Judith were more like cross-examinations. Judith was constantly pumping her for information.

Maria was promoted to customer relations manager. Several times, during the week her new position was announced, all conversation stopped when Maria entered the employee lounge. Maria decided to ask Judith what the problem was.

"What am I doing wrong, Judith? Do people really resent me that much? I'm only doing the best job I know how; I didn't try to take this promotion away from Bill. Do people think I stole it from him? Is that the problem?"

Judith looked embarrassed. "Well, Maria, maybe I shouldn't tell you this, but the rumor is that you and Lee are more than co-workers. That's why you've been promoted, not Bill. Everyone thinks Lee is playing favorites."

Maria was shocked. "Judith, you know that's not true! Didn't you tell them the truth?"

Judith stammered, "What could I say? You told me yourself you thought Lee was very nice and that the two of you worked so well together."

Maria shook her head. "I thought you were my friend. I guess I was wrong."

Your Analysis

Characterize Maria's attitude toward her job. What did Maria do to feed the rumor mill at work? Was she wrong?

_____

_____

Characterize Judith's attitude toward her job. What was Judith's role in this situation?

_____

_____

Did Judith's actions increase or decrease morale and productivity?

_____

_____

Concepts

Communication plays a vital role in all our interactions. It is human nature to want to share information with others. We share our joys and sorrows, our successes and failures, our hopes and fears with our families, friends, and even relative strangers. It is impossible to spend several hours a day with other people, whether at home, at school, or at work, and not share some of ourselves with them through conversation.

This sharing of information can have positive or negative results. It is as easy to pass along misinformation as information. Misinformation is untrue or incomplete information that can have serious negative consequences.

How Rumors Work

Rumors are often based on misinformation. A rumor is a piece of information of great interest to a group of people. Because so many people are interested in the subject matter of rumors, they spread quickly. Frequently, they become distorted as they spread.

For example, a worker may overhear two supervisors discussing a possible layoff of one part-time employee. He repeats this to a co-worker, who then repeats it to a third party. By the time worker number four spreads the message, it becomes "All part-timers will be laid off."

Before the end of the week, the rumor of major layoffs in every department is making the rounds. Naturally, everyone who hears such a rumor is worried that his or her job may be affected. Productivity declines as workers worry about their future. They bring that worry home with them in the evening. One rumor can negatively affect a large group of people.

Maria's relationships with her co-workers are negatively affected by rumors. Her department is suffering from low morale as a result of those rumors. Maria's happiness in her new promotion has been tainted by the attitude of those she works with.

Maria has made a couple of mistakes. In her enthusiasm to share Lee's positive comments, she may have chosen the wrong person to tell. Judith and Bill have been co-workers for a long time. Judith feels loyalty to Bill, and this loyalty may influence her reaction to Judith's news. Judith cannot wait to tell Bill what Maria said. And Bill, who wants the promotion for himself, is threatened. The rumor mill begins to turn out reasons for Maria's success.

Maria also discovered that Judith cannot keep a secret. This is not unusual; everyone has had the experience of telling something confidential and regretting it later. The best approach is simply this: If you do not want confidential information to become common knowledge, do not share it with anyone. Rumormongers love secrets.

Avoid Negative Comments

Examine your motives when telling someone something, especially something negative. "If you can't say something nice, don't say anything" is old advice, but still true. Think of the rumors you have heard—very few are positive.

Rumors grow from negative comments about co-workers, about supervisors, or about jobs and positions. When you talk, remember that everything you say will probably be repeated. Do not say anything you would be embarrassed to have attributed to you.

Consider the Source

When you hear negative comments, examine the motives of the teller. When Judith warned Maria not to get her hopes up about the promotion, what were her motives? Did she want to warn Maria of a real problem? Or was her loyalty to Bill leading her to say things that would lessen Maria's happiness? Maria needed to examine Judith's comments about Lee in the same way. If Maria had accepted what Judith said about Lee, it could have undermined her ability to work with him and her performance on the job. Eventually, it could even have cost her the promotion.

Change the Subject

Employees with constructive attitudes will be less likely to pass rumors. Loyalty to an employer or to the company will make them less likely to pass along unsubstantiated or negative information. When co-workers gossip, do not join in. Change the subject to your hobby, sports, or last night's television shows.

Negative talk, like a negative attitude, is destructive. The rumor mill can make even the best job in the world an unhappy one.

Review

Consider the answers you gave before reading the concepts. If you feel that you understood the situation and are satisfied with your first answer, write "no change" on the line. If you feel you have new insights or understanding, write your new answer or additional information.

Characterize Maria's attitude toward her job. What did Maria do to feed the rumor mill at work? Was she wrong?

_____

_____

Characterize Judith's attitude toward her job. What was Judith's role in this situation?

_____

_____

Did Judith's actions increase or decrease morale and productivity?

_____

_____

Discussion

1. Describe the impact of rumors on the job.

_____

_____

_____

2. What role does attitude play in the development and
   passing of rumors?

_____

_____

_____

3. Identify a situation in school or at work when you suc-
   cessfully maintained a constructive attitude and avoided
   gossiping.

_____

_____

_____

ACCEPTING RESPONSIBILITY

Case Study 11
Accepting Responsibility

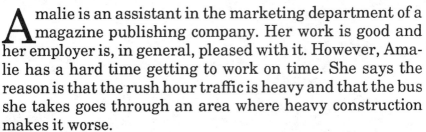

After completing this unit, you will:

☐ Recognize how accepting responsibility is an important human relations skill.

☐ Identify a time in your own experience at work or in class when you found it was better to accept responsibility.

Amalie is an assistant in the marketing department of a magazine publishing company. Her work is good and her employer is, in general, pleased with it. However, Amalie has a hard time getting to work on time. She says the reason is that the rush hour traffic is heavy and that the bus she takes goes through an area where heavy construction makes it worse.

Since she was a small child she has had difficulty getting started in the morning. She likes the evening and usually stays up late. She often goes out to the movies or parties. When she does not go out, she stays up late reading and watching television.

After often arriving at 9:00 instead of 8:30, when she is supposed to, Amalie is called into her manager's office. Her manager wants Amalie to be there at 8:30 but does not want to discourage her, because her work otherwise is good. The manager points out that it is not fair to the others in the department who start working half an hour earlier than Amalie.

Amalie suggests that perhaps she could work half an hour later each day with the understanding that she will start half an hour later in the morning. Her boss asks if she thinks she will be punctual and always be in at 9:00 sharp. Amalie says yes. So they agree to the new schedule.

For two weeks Amalie is at work every day at 9. Gradually, however, she starts coming in later until she is regularly getting in at 9:20 or 9:30. She realizes that the traffic is still bad at the later hour and that she does not like getting up at the later hour any more than at the earlier hour.

After six weeks, Amalie's manager calls her into the office again. Amalie tells her boss that the traffic is worse at the later hour but it gets better after that. She suggests that she come in at 9:30 and leave at 5:30.

Her boss says absolutely not.

He points out that he had been willing to give Amalie six weeks to try the new schedule and it did not work. Now, he says, she must come in at 8:30 as do the others. Amalie's boss makes a note in her personnel file to monitor her. He warns her of possibly being put on probation and says that there will be no raises or a promotion until Amalie shows she can be relied on.

Your Analysis

Explain the outcome:

_____

_____

Evaluate the outcome:

_____

_____

Would you change it if you could?

_____

_____

How would you change it?

_____

_____

Concepts

Is the ability to accept responsibility for yourself a human relations skill? It is. You are interacting with others all the time, whether or not you are deliberately communicating. What you do or fail to do affects others one way or another. If even your moods can have an effect on others, your actions assuredly can.

A person unwilling or unable to accept responsibility for what she or he does will have poor human relations. Perhaps you have known someone who did not accept responsibility and was always looking for excuses.

Oh, that sweater you loaned me got stained. Betty hit my arm while I was drinking coffee.

No, I didn't finish the report. People kept interrupting me.

I didn't do the job right, because you didn't explain it clearly.

I would have done it better if you had let me do it my way.

I don't know what happened to it; it's just gone.

You can probably think of other examples. The point is, how do people like that make you feel? Eager to loan them things, help them out, work with them? No. People who cannot take responsibility for their actions annoy and irritate those with whom they interact. Soon, others shun them.

Admit Mistakes

Accepting responsibility is closely related to other human relations skills, such as the ability to admit a mistake. To exercise responsibility often requires that you have a sound knowledge of yourself and an ability to assess your strengths and weaknesses.

Accepting responsibility does not mean that you have to go around confessing, but it does require you to be aware of yourself. It requires that you be aware of what type of person you are and, if you cannot change something about yourself, that you adjust your life accordingly. There is an old plea that goes:

> *Give me the courage to change those things that I can change, the serenity to accept those things that I cannot change, and the wisdom to know the difference.*

It is easy, of course, to accept responsibility when things go well. The person with good human relations has the skill and the knowledge to be able to accept responsibility when the situation is less positive. Doing so is good human relations in its own right because people respect and admire this trait. Furthermore, accepting responsibility is also the first step toward correcting whatever the problem might be.

Review

Consider the answers you gave before reading the concepts. If you feel that you understood the situation and are satisfied with your first answer, write "no change" on the line. If you feel you have new insights or understanding, write your new answer or additional information.

Explain the outcome:

_____

_____

Evaluate the outcome:

_____

_____

Would you change it if you could?

_____

_____

How would you change it?

_____

_____

Discussion

1. In your own words, explain how accepting responsibility for one's actions is a human relations skill.

_____

_____

_____

2. From your own experience, give an example of why it was better to accept responsibility for an action than to avoid taking responsibility.

_____

_____

_____

Case Study

12

COMMUNICATION

Case Study 12
Communication

After completing this chapter, you will:

☐ Recognize the importance of good communication skills in building relationships in the workplace.

☐ Identify three types of verbal communication.

☐ Identify several kinds of nonverbal communication.

☐ Identify an incident where your positive attitude played an effective role in your communications.

The medical benefits office of Akron Automobiles was one of the busiest departments at the huge plant. With more than 15,000 employees to service, the office was a place of nonstop activity. Each insurance clerk was responsible for completing numerous claim forms and mailing out payment checks to doctors, hospitals, and the employees themselves. A steady stream of workers with questions and a constantly ringing telephone added to the confusion.

Tyrone was swamped with past-due insurance claims. On top of that, he had been assigned to train Francine, the newly hired clerk. It was only Monday morning, and already Tyrone was sure this would be a terrible week.

Tyrone was immersed in his work, unraveling a complicated claim, when Francine arrived. Tyrone looked up from his work with a loud sigh and acknowledged her greeting with a curt nod. He was obviously annoyed at the interruption. He sat at his desk, staring at Francine and waiting for her to talk, tapping his pencil impatiently on the desk.

Francine, already anxious about the size of the office and the complex new job, filled the silence with nervous chatter. Finally, Tyrone leaned back in his chair, arms folded, and said, "I'm much too busy for this. I was ordered to train you, and I will, but I really don't want to know your life's history."

Francine was mortified. She had wanted to make a good impression, and now this person thought she was an idiot. In a whisper, with reddened cheeks, Francine apologized.

Tyrone resolved to get this training over as soon as possible. He launched into a complicated explanation of the tasks involved. His tone of voice communicated his annoyance. Francine tried her best to understand what he was saying, but he kept jumping from topic to topic. When she interrupted to ask questions, his look told her that she was brainless for not understanding in the first place. Francine's self-confidence was deserting her.

The phone rang often. Tyrone had no more time for the people calling with questions than he had for Francine. He answered the phone with a curt "Yes?" and his manner was abrupt. At least, Francine thought, it's not just me.

As the morning progressed, Francine felt more and more lost. She tried to tell Tyrone, but he was not listening. He never made eye contact with her.

Francine had arrived, head high and smiling, a bit nervous but excited about starting a job with greater responsibility. As she left at the end of the day, her shoulders were hunched and her head down. The excitement was gone.

Your Analysis

What type of verbal and nonverbal communication did Tyrone employ?

_____

_____

What role did Tyrone's attitude play in his communication with Francine?

_____

_____

Analyze the outcome. Do you think Tyrone and Francine can build a mutually rewarding relationship?

_____

_____

Concepts

Communication and attitude are two of the most important factors in success—both individual success and company success. The best product in the world will go unsold if the seller cannot communicate with the buyer. The most needed services will not be used if the attitude of the service provider is poor.

Communication skills are often divided into verbal communication and nonverbal communication.

Verbal Communication

Verbal communication includes all the ways that you interact with others through words. Whether spoken face to face, delivered over the telephone, or transmitted in writing, words provide us with an important ability to be understood. Verbal communication involves the words you use and the effectiveness with which you state your message. The vocabulary and grammar you use, your pronunciation, your tone of voice, the way you organize your thoughts, all affect the message others hear. Tyrone's poor communication skills almost guarantee that Francine will not understand her new job.

Good communication skills over the telephone are important, also. Because your listener has no visual cues to help in understanding you, clear verbal communication is essential. Allowing long silences, nodding your head, or mumbling into the receiver will result in poor communication. Your tone of voice will convey to callers whether you are happy to help them or annoyed at their calls.

Clarity and organization are important to your written communication skills also. Memos, reports, even a simple telephone message should be clear, complete, and free of jargon or inaccuracy. Many people who communicate well with spoken words have trouble expressing themselves on paper. There are many excellent books on business communication and correspondence written to help develop your skill in written communication. One tip is to imagine yourself speaking to one person as you write. Explain your problem or directions to that one person.

Nonverbal Communication

The way you communicate nonverbally is as important as verbal communication. If verbal communication refers to communication with words, then nonverbal communication includes everything else you do to communicate. Body language refers to your hand gestures, facial expressions, posture, and position when you are speaking or listening.

When you interact with others, do you smile or frown? When listening in class, are you sitting alertly or slumped in your seat with your head in your hands. Look around the room. What nonverbal messages can you read in the posture of the other students? Of the teacher? Making eye contact and smiling lets others know we are interested in talking to them or listening to what they have to say.

Two-Way Street

Communication is a two-way street. Getting your message across is one part; listening to the other person is the rest. The goal of communication is to establish a relationship with another person. To do this, you need to hear what they are saying. Be aware of others' verbal and nonverbal communication cues.

When you listen to a speaker in a lecture, or on the radio or television, how effectively does he or she communicate? Recall the last time you heard an interesting lecture. The speaker who interested you was undoubtedly interested in and excited by the topic. His enthusiastic attitude was communicated to you through his words and body language. You responded positively to that enthusiasm.

Tyrone's poor attitude toward training Francine was evident through his verbal communication (tone of voice, choice of words, lack of clarity) and his nonverbal communication (folded arms, tapping pencil, lack of eye contact). His attitude toward interruptions was evident in his poor communication skills over the telephone. In his desire to do his work quickly and efficiently, Tyrone was forgetting that his job involved people as well as paperwork.

Good communication skills and good human relations skills go hand in hand. Your attitude influences the way you communicate; the way you communicate with others affects their opinion of you and influences their attitude toward you.

Co-workers who can communicate effectively will find that they can work together better. This will increase group productivity and enhance the work environment.

Review

Consider the answers you gave before reading the concepts. If you feel that you understood the situation and are satisfied with your first answer, write "no change" on the line. If you feel you have new insights or understanding, write your new answer or additional information.

What type of verbal and nonverbal communication did Tyrone employ?

_____

_____

What role did Tyrone's attitude play in his communication with Francine? ˙˙

_____

_____

Analyze the outcome. Do you think Tyrone and Francine can build a working relationship?

_____

_____

Discussion

1. Why are good communication skills important in building relationships in the workplace?

_____

_____

_____

2. Describe three types of verbal communication.

_____

_____

_____

3. Give examples of different types of nonverbal communication.

_____

_____

_____

4. What role does attitude play in communication?

_____

_____

_____

YOUR ATTITUDE AND JOB SUCCESS

Case Study 13

Your Attitude and Job Success

After completing this chapter, you will:

- ☐ Identify traits that form a constructive attitude.

- ☐ Recognize the role of a constructive attitude in career success.

Jacob Spivack is one of Perfect Printers' most successful sales representatives. Because of his good performance record, he was assigned to train Martha O'Brien, the newest member of the sales team. Martha was looking forward to learning Jacob's secrets of success.

Martha was surprised when she first met Jacob. She had expected to meet an outgoing, aggressive salesman, self-assured and maybe even a bit pushy. Jacob was soft-spoken and very different from Martha's stereotypical view of the successful sales rep. In fact, some of the other men and women in the department seemed as if they would be better salespeople.

What Martha learned was surprising. Jacob had no high-powered philosophy of sales. He liked what he did. He believed that Perfect Printers offered the best quality services at competitive prices. He saw his job as a chance to introduce others to that service.

Jacob was greeted with pleasure by the business owners he contacted. Martha noticed how he seemed to know enough about each person or business in his territory to suggest just the right product or service. He never failed to ask if his clients were pleased with their last order.

Jacob's customers were happy and recommended him and Perfect Printers to their friends. Jacob expanded his client list each week as he followed through on these leads. When a lead was in a co-worker's territory, Jacob always passed it on. Knowing how competitive many top salespeople were, Martha asked Jacob why he would do this. Jacob seemed surprised at her question. After all, more customers meant more business and higher profits for Perfect Printers.

A problem arose one day over a large shipment that was delayed. Unfortunately, it was one of Jacob's newest accounts. The owner, Mr. Marley, was upset and took out his anger and frustration on Jacob. Martha expected Jacob to place the blame where it belonged, on the shipping department. He did not. Jacob made no excuses, only apologies. He arranged for the shipment, which had been misplaced, to be delivered by the close of business that day. Mr. Marley realized that he had treated Jacob unfairly. He was impressed with Jacob's calm and competent response. He told Jacob that he would give Perfect Printers another chance.

Martha trained with Jacob for a month. On several days, she noticed he seemed quieter than usual. When she asked what was bothering him, Jacob told her that his apartment was being converted to condominiums and he had to move. He was worried about finding another affordable apartment on short notice. Martha admired his ability to do his job when faced with personal problems. His clients were never aware that Jacob had anything on his mind but their needs.

Your Analysis

How would you characterize Jacob's attitude toward his job?

_____

_____

What attitudes made Jacob a valuable employee?

_____

_____

Will training with Jacob make Martha a better sales rep? Why or why not?

_____

_____

Do you predict career success and advancement for Jacob?

_____

_____

Concepts

The valued employee has a constructive attitude toward the job, co-workers, customers, and supervisors. Good human relations skills combined with a positive attitude are essential to success in any career you choose. Let's examine the traits that form the attitude of a valuable worker.

Dependability

Dependability is an asset in all your relationships. When you are dependable, customers know that you will provide good products and services. Your co-workers know that you will do your share of a job. They will not need to cover for you or do extra work.

Loyalty

Loyalty is as important in working relationships as in personal ones. Loyalty to your company means that you will not make negative comments about the company and its product. Loyalty to co-workers means that you will not contribute to the rumor mill with unsubstantiated gossip or speculation about a fellow employee.

If you have a problem with a supervisor, loyalty to the person and the position requires you to take your problem directly to him or her, rather than make disparaging comments to others. Personal loyalty ensures that you will remain true to your ideals if asked to do something unethical or dishonest.

Honesty

Honesty is an important element of the ideal employee. Stealing from your employer can be obvious—taking money or items of inventory, including office supplies—are less obvious. Stealing time is a factor in decreased productivity.

Ten minutes late in the morning, an extra coffee break, 15 extra minutes at lunch—all this steals productive worktime from your company. Receiving or making long personal phone calls is another theft of time—and if they are long-distance calls, that is a theft of money. Unauthorized use of the copy machine is a problem in some workplaces.

Conscientiousness

Supervisors look for a conscientious attitude in their workers. The conscientious worker performs whether supervised or not. Doing the job as well as possible is important. Conscientious workers learn what is expected of them and can be counted on to do it. Their horizontal and vertical relationships are enhanced because supervisors and co-workers know they will pull their weight.

The person who demonstrates dependability, loyalty, honesty, and conscientiousness in business dealings is halfway to success. Personal integrity is never wasted. In the job world, however, just being a good person may not be enough. You need to combine integrity and a constructive attitude with initiative.

Initiative

The employee with initiative does that little bit extra. The secretary with initiative enrolls in a computer course and learns a new skill. When the office computer is installed, she will be ready to use it.

Perfect Printers is lucky to have Jacob as a sales representative. His personal qualities and constructive attitude are an asset to their business. Try to imagine Jacob being consistently late for work or failing to show for an appointment. Can you picture him joining in gossip about another employee or running down Perfect Printers' products to a customer? Jacob's human relations skills will take him far.

Review

Consider the answers you gave before reading the concepts. If you feel that you understood the situation and are satisfied with your first answer, write "no change" on the line. If you feel you have new insights or understanding, write your new answer or additional information.

How would you characterize Jacob's attitude toward his job?

_____

_____

What attitudes made Jacob a valuable employee?

_____

_____

Will training with Jacob make Martha a better sales rep? Why or why not?

_____

_____

Do you predict career success and advancement for Jacob?

_____

_____

Discussion

1. Identify five personal traits of yours that you feel give you a constructive attitude.

_____

_____

_____

2. How has a positive, constructive attitude made you more successful in school or work?

_____

_____

_____

Maintaining a Positive Attitude

Case Study 14
Maintaining a Positive Attitude

After completing this chapter, you will:

- ☐ Identify strategies you have used for maintaining a positive attitude.

- ☐ Identify a situation either at work or at school where an attitude resulted in good human relations skills.

Pamela Jakes, nurse's aide, arrived at Greenwood Nursing Home 15 minutes early for her 3 p.m. to 11 p.m. shift. Those extra few minutes gave her time to talk to the aide she would be replacing. She could find out whether any of the patients on her floor were having difficulty. Sometimes, patient problems during the day meant that some of the duties of the day shift had to be handled in the evening. Today was one of those days. Pamela received a quick briefing and planned how she would organize her time to fit in everything that needed to be done.

As Pamela entered the coatroom, Maggie called to her. Pamela waved hello, but kept on walking. Maggie, the senior aide on the evening shift, always had a complaint. As Pamela walked down the hall, Maggie caught up to her.

"It's just you and me tonight, again," Maggie complained. "That darn Anna called in. One of her kids has the flu and she couldn't take her to the sitter's. I'm getting sick and tired of this! I'll bet it's just an excuse to see that boyfriend of hers. I'll tell you..."

Pamela cut her short, trying to keep the irritation out of her voice. "Anna rarely takes time off, Maggie. Why would you doubt her excuse? It's hard raising three young kids alone, and I admire her for working so hard to support them. Besides, the flu can be dangerous to an elderly person. Anna should stay home rather than take the chance of spreading infection."

"Just makes more work for us," Maggie grumbled. But the complaints stopped.

Pamela started the evening routine. Many of her patients were glad to see her. She always had a pleasant greeting. She asked about their families and their health. Pamela was efficient but never brusque. When she had the time, she spent a few extra minutes, giving a backrub or reviewing last night's television shows. Pamela knew that many of these people rarely had visitors. Conversation and touching were important to them.

Some patients were ill and in pain, or senile. Some were just cantankerous. They would yell at her or blame her for their problems. When she tried to take care of their physical needs, they would refuse to cooperate, sometimes yanking her arm or pushing her away.

Pamela often heard Maggie yell back. Pamela remembered that their anger was not directed at her personally. She knew they were angry at their illness and their inability to cope. Pamela tried to put herself in their place. She treated all her patients as she would want to be treated.

Joan, the registered nurse in charge of the floor, spent precious time checking that Maggie's work was completed. She knew that Pamela would do what was needed—and more—without her direct supervision. Joan considered Pamela her right arm. Pamela had volunteered to attend in-service training sessions on her own time. She had asked to borrow Joan's nursing journals and health magazines to read. Joan encouraged Pamela to attend nursing school— she would be an excellent nurse.

Your Analysis

How would you characterize Pamela's attitude toward her job?

_____

_____

List the constructive attitudes she displays.

_____

_____

What strategies does Pamela use to maintain a positive attitude in difficult situations?

_____

_____

Concepts

Perhaps, somewhere in the world, there is a person who is constantly in a positive frame of mind. This person has a perfect job and an ideal homelife. Every day is wonderful. Perhaps this person truly exists, but it is not likely.

Everyone's life—home, school, and work—is full of ups and downs, positive and negative situations. Having effective strategies to use in maintaining a positive attitude will help you to cope with these situations.

Strategy Number 1

The first, and most important, strategy is to examine your attitude regularly. Ask yourself:

Am I practicing good human relations skills?

What is my attitude toward my job?

Is it constructive or destructive?

Consider all aspects, including your relationships with your co-workers and with your supervisors.

If your attitude is negative, ask yourself why?

Am I unsuited for my job?

Are personal problems interfering with my work performance?

Do I dislike my co-workers or supervisor?

Do I need more training to perform my tasks effectively?

How can I change destructive attitudes to constructive ones?

If you feel that your attitude is positive, are you projecting that attitude to others?

*How do you think your supervisor would character-
ize you?*

*How would your co-workers rate your human rela-
tions skills? Be honest!*

Most likely, you will discover one or two areas where you
need to adjust your attitude. You may love your job but find
dealing with certain customers exasperating. That exasper-
ation will show in your attitude. Recognizing that there is
a problem, you can work to fix it. Having specific strategies
to use in maintaining a positive attitude is a big help.

Strategy Number 2

Try to achieve a balance between your personal life and your
career. Only you can decide what is the more important
priority in your life. Once you have identified your needs
and priorities, you can strike a balance that works for you.
When you are at home, concentrate on your family and
friends. Leave work problems at work.

Similarly, when at work, put home problems on a back
burner. Resolve to concentrate on matters at hand. If you
know that you have ordered your life in the best way for
yourself, a positive attitude toward work will follow.

Strategy Number 3

Focus on the positive. When one aspect of your job gets you
down, do not let it get out of hand. Pamela could focus on
her difficult patients and the unpleasant aspects of dealing
with them. Eventually, this negative attitude would be
communicated to all her patients. Instead, Pamela concen-
trates on the good she accomplishes. She reminds herself of
the importance of her voice, her touch, her interest, and her
skill to the lonely and bedridden.

Focus on the positive in your relationships at work as
well. Remember, you can have an effective working relationship even with those who have a different set of personal

values. Concentrate on the values and goals you share, such as building a productive department.

Strategy Number 4

Communicate. Communication is our link with others. When you feel isolated or cut off, at home or at work, your lines of communication need to be repaired. It's hard to keep a positive attitude if you feel misunderstood.

Practice good listening and communication skills every day. Be sure that you say what you mean and that you hear what others are saying. Ask questions if you are unsure of directions. If you are giving directions, be sure your listeners know what to do.

Strategy Number 5

Turn changes into opportunities. Humans are creatures of habit. It is the rare person who likes changes. We are comfortable with the familiar—familiar friends, supervisors, and co-workers, familiar routines, familiar foods. However, change is an inevitable part of life, particularly your work life. Companies are bought and sold and management changes, bringing change to all departments. Co-workers and supervisors come and go. Your duties change. New company policies go into effect.

Your first reaction to changes at work may be apprehension or dismay. However, you can overcome your initial fear if you see these changes as a chance to stretch yourself, to prove yourself. Every new situation can be a learning experience if you are open to learning. Adopt the attitude that every change presents a unique opportunity to grow.

Strategy Number 6

Educate yourself. It's tough to maintain a positive attitude if you are struggling to understand your job. Education is the key to achieving confidence in your abilities. You may choose to pursue your education by taking traditional courses. You can also keep abreast of changes in your field by reading trade publications and new books by experts in the field. Pamela pursued her education in both ways, by taking in-service training and by reading medical journals.

Education is necessary for advancement in many careers. Even if that is not the case, education is never wasted. The more you learn, the more confident you will be.

Strategy Number 7

Boost your initiative. In the first months on a job, you may find yourself looking for ways to improve your productivity and performance. The excitement and challenge you feel are reflected in your attitude.

As time goes on, it's natural for this enthusiasm to die down a bit. You may find that you do only as much as needed to keep your job, and only when told. If you find your enthusiasm flagging, look for ways to revive the challenge you once felt. Analyze your job responsibilities, and look for opportunities to show initiative and ambition.

Supervisors count on workers with initiative and enthusiasm to show new employees the ropes. If Joan was looking for an employee to train a newly hired aide, do you think she would ask Pamela or Maggie? Maggie may be the senior aide at Greenwood, but she has long ago lost any enthusiasm she had for the job. Her negative attitude affects her relationships with the patients, supervisors, and other aides.

Strategy Number 8

Maintain a sense of humor. Humor can help you put situations in perspective. Taking yourself and others too seriously will not solve problems, and it may cause you to dwell on mistakes or focus on the negative side of situations that cannot be changed. Developing a sense of humor does not mean becoming the office clown. It does mean developing the ability to see the lighter side of situations.

Strategy Number 9

Take care of your health. Poor health habits will affect your job performance and your outlook—perhaps not immediately, but over time.

An occasional candy bar for lunch will not ruin your health, but a steady diet of junk food will sap your energy. Staying up too late every night will affect your ability to remain alert the next day.

A lack of exercise may result in a buildup of tensions and lack of stamina.

Abuse of alcohol and drugs will certainly not improve your attitude.

Strategy Number 10

Dress for success. You may think that attitude relates only to your frame of mind. However, it is more complex. Your attitude and your appearance are related. If you look good, you are more likely to feel good about yourself.

Everyone has a favorite outfit that can improve a mood just by being put on. You may like the color or style, or just feel that it flatters you. Choose that outfit to wear in stressful situations because knowing you look good boosts your confidence.

Your appearance also affects others' opinions of you and their reactions to you. Demonstrate a positive attitude by paying attention to personal hygiene and grooming. Dress appropriately for the position you hold.

Review

Consider the answers you gave before reading the concepts. If you feel that you understood the situation and are satisfied with your first answer, write "no change" on the line. If you feel you have new insights or understanding, write your new answer or additional information.

How would you characterize Pamela's attitude toward her job?

_____

_____

List the constructive attitudes she displays.

_____

_____

What strategies does Pamela use to maintain a positive attitude in difficult situations?

_____

_____

Discussion

1. Identify five to eight strategies that you developed to maintain a positive attitude.

_____

_____

_____

2. Review the importance of maintaining a positive attitude and practicing good human relations skills on the job.

_____

_____

_____

3. Give an example from your own experience where you needed to maintain a positive attitude. What strategies did you use?

_____

_____

_____

SUCCEEDING IN A
NEW JOB

Case Study 15

Succeeding in a New Job

MORNING!

After completing this chapter, you will:

☐ Recognize that testing is frequently part of initiation into a new group.

☐ Identify the strategies you have developed to cope with a new situation.

Erica Porter had waited for months to be transferred from the maintenance crew to the kitchen staff at Community Hospital. Finally, the transfer came. Erica expected the transition to the kitchen to be easy. After all, she knew many of the workers from coffee breaks.

Erica had no problem learning the job. She was familiar with the hospital layout. Faced with five floors, two wings, and more than 150 rooms, many new employees became lost while delivering and collecting meal trays.

Erica arrived in the kitchen Monday, dressed in her new uniform, eager to begin. Everyone greeted her pleasantly and the morning passed quickly. At break time she hoped to sit with her new co-workers, but no one asked her to. Instead, her old friends from Maintenance hailed her, and so she sat with them.

The newest workers were given the least-liked assignment. This was not unusual—she remembered scrubbing toilets for a month before a newly hired maintenance worker relieved her. In the kitchen, she was given the least-liked job of unloading the tray carts after meals.

Erica expected that. What she did not expect were the comments. The other workers seemed to have opinions about everything Erica did—from the way she scraped the trays to how she did her hair, from the type of sneakers she wore to her former job. None of the comments were good. Erica tried to laugh them off, but some really stung.

Friday was the worst day. One solid week of being odd-one-out in such a tightly knit group was wearing Erica down. When her supervisor asked how she liked the job, Erica could barely choke out the words "It's fine."

Friday was Erica's day to stay late. She had noticed during the week that everyone pitched in to help so that the late person was not held up any longer than necessary. Erica had pitched in, too. She expected them to help her in return.

But instead of helping her finish her work, Erica's co-workers stood around watching her, commenting on how slow she was. When she asked someone to hand her the tray in the hall, she was told, "It's not my job. Get it yourself." Erica's shoulders slumped as she went to get the tray.

All weekend, Erica dreaded returning to work. She could not imagine what she had done to deserve such treatment. She wondered if she should confront them with her feelings.

Erica discussed her problem with Phil, her boyfriend. He advised her to hang in there. He told her how the other packers had treated him when he first joined the loading dock. Now, they were all great buddies. Erica decided to wait a little longer before confronting her co-workers.

The second week was much the same, except for one bright spot. She worked closely with LaDonna, who did not join in the teasing. Erica felt she and LaDonna might become friends.

Gradually, the teasing lessened. One day, after Erica's third week on the job, LaDonna invited Erica to sit with the kitchen workers during break. The others asked Erica about her family and her life outside of work. It was the first time anyone had showed a personal interest in her.

Your Analysis

Why was Erica ostracized and teased by the other workers?

_____

_____

Should she have confronted them with her feelings?

_____

_____

What strategies could Erica have used to succeed in her new job?

_____

_____

Concepts

Starting a new job is a stressful time. On the one hand, it is exciting and exhilarating to meet new people and learn new skills. On the other hand, it is human nature to be apprehensive of new situations and worried about failing.

Good human relations skills can ease your entry into a new job or position. A positive attitude will help as you establish new horizontal and vertical relationships. The important thing to remember is to be patient.

A Time of Testing

You are the newcomer, joining a group that may be long established. Employees who have established relationships and a hierarchy among themselves may see you as the intruder. They need time to see whether you are going to fit in with the group. Are you going to make their jobs easier? Or will your arrival mean more work for them?

If you join a fraternity or sorority, there is often a period of initiation. It is a time of testing, to see whether you can be one of a special group. Some of the testing can be cruel.

Erica's co-workers were putting her through a period of initiation, also. They needed to test her skills and see whether she would fit in with their group. They may not have been consciously aware of this; they might even be surprised to have it pointed out to them.

Phil gave Erica good advice. The best way to deal with this testing is to wait it out. If you know that it is a ritual that almost every new employee endures, you can wait for it to end.

Confronting the others may mean that you will never be accepted as part of the group.

Reacting with anger or running to your supervisor for help can damage the development of working relationships.

Few Pats on the Back

If this is your first job, there is something else you should realize. In many work situations, feedback on your performance is rare. Praise or feedback is not freely given by co-workers or supervisors.

Students entering the workforce for the first time, used to praise and other feedback for their work from teachers and parents, may have a hard time realizing this. In many job situations, the only time you will receive a comment on your performance is when you make a mistake!

How to Survive

How can you survive this period of teasing and testing with your attitude intact? Do your job to the best of your ability. Watch what others do, and ask questions if there is something you do not understand. You may be teased at first, but your co-workers will appreciate your efforts to improve the productivity of the group.

Send out positive verbal and nonverbal signals. Let the others know that, when they are ready, you are open to friendly overtures. Often, the shy or quiet new employee will be seen as stuck-up. Be aware of the signals you are giving off.

Learn the Rules

Learn the written and unwritten rules of the workplace. If your company has an employee handbook, read it. If there is an unwritten policy that your co-workers follow, try to decipher it from their behavior. For example, Erica realized that it was an unwritten rule that all the kitchen workers help the person assigned to late duty. By joining in, Erica showed that she was willing to play by the team rules.

Some new employees may face harsher tests. This is especially true when someone is stretching the boundaries that have existed for centuries.

For example, the woman who joins a typically male work environment, such as construction or fire fighting, may find her ability to perform questioned. It may take her longer to be accepted as part of the group. Similarly, a man in a traditionally female role, such as nurse or childcare provider, may find his motives and masculinity questioned.

The reasons for testing newcomers, seeing whether they are worthy to be a part of the group, has forever been a part of human behavior. As long as it does not become a means of excluding those who are different, it can be overcome. You can survive your initiation and go on to forge strong relationships.

Review

Consider the answers you gave before reading the concepts. If you feel that you understood the situation and are satisfied with your first answer, write "no change" on the line. If you feel you have new insights or understanding, write your new answer or additional information.

Why was Erica ostracized and teased by the other workers?

_____

_____

Should she have confronted them with her feelings?

_____

_____

What strategies could Erica have used to succeed in her new job?

_____

_____

Discussion

1. Identify the testing you experienced as a new employee, new in a class, or a new club member.

_____

_____

_____

2. Identify strategies you developed to cope with testing and to maintain a positive attitude.

_____

_____

_____

Case Study 16

Absenteeism and Tardiness

After completing this chapter, you will:

☐ Recognize attitudes that contribute to absenteeism and tardiness.

☐ Identify the negative impact of absenteeism and tardiness on the job.

☐ Identify ways to avoid absenteeism and tardiness.

Nelson Carmichael rushed through the front door of Robertson Electronics. In his haste, he narrowly avoided colliding with a customer on his way out. Ralph Robertson stood inside the door, arms crossed, looking very displeased.

"I'm really sorry, Mr. Robertson." Nelson tried to catch his breath. "It's just that my alarm didn't go off and..."

"Save the explanation—I'm not interested," Mr. Robertson replied. "Did you recognize that customer you almost knocked over as you raced in?"

"I guess I didn't really notice...oh, no!" Nelson smacked his head. "I forgot! I was going to show Mrs. Hunter that new stereo system we just got in stock."

"Well, she was here right on time," Mr. Reynolds said. "When I explained that you weren't here and the display model was still crated downstairs, she left. Didn't I ask you to assemble that system the day before yesterday when I left for Boston? What happened?"

Uh, oh, Nelson thought. Now I'm in for it. "I...I was tied up with customers all morning. And then, well, I guess I left a little early."

"How early is a little early?" Mr. Roberts asked. "Ten minutes? Two hours?"

"It's just that I had these tickets to the game, and with the traffic and all I wanted to get good seats." Even as he said it, Nelson knew he was in big trouble this time.

"Nelson, you are my most knowledgeable salesman. I rely on your technical expertise. When you are here, you are my top salesman. But that's the problem...you're almost never here! I was looking over your records—you are late almost half the time. And I can count on you missing work entirely at least once every two weeks. Do you realize that in the past three months, you've called in sick on six Mondays and twice on Friday?

"I think my policies on absenteeism and tardiness are pretty liberal. I know my employees have lives outside of this building, and I try to make allowances for that. But you have abused my generosity.

"Nelson, I really hate to do this, but I'm afraid you are on probation. If I don't see a definite improvement in your attendance record this month, I will have to replace you."

Your Analysis

Is Ralph Robertson justified in criticizing Nelson?

_____

_____

What effect do Nelson's absenteeism and tardiness have on his job? On Robertson Electronics?

_____

_____

How do you think Nelson's attitude will affect the other employees?

_____

_____

Concepts

Absenteeism and tardiness of employees cause problems for all business owners. Whether the business is a huge manufacturing plant or a small store like Robertson Electronics, business owners know that they must have policies in place to deal with workers who abuse sick leave and arrival and departure times.

A Costly Practice

Absenteeism and tardiness cost businesses money. Being five minutes late for work occasionally may not be a problem. Imagine, however, if you were five minutes late for work every day. If your wage is $10 an hour, your tardiness costs your employer roughly 83 cents a day. Over a year, your chronic tardiness costs more than $200! Now, imagine that 20 employees are five minutes late every day. The business is losing $4,150 a year due to tardiness.

Tardiness and absenteeism steal productive time from your employer.

If you are consistently late or often absent from work, your co-workers have to pick up the slack—they will have to do their own jobs and cover for you as well. Once or twice, this may not cause any problems, but if it happens often, your co-workers will resent it.

One worker's tardiness or absenteeism causes stress for the other employees; there is tension in the department.

Supervisors are unhappy if one or more employees are chronically absent or tardy. And an unhappy supervisor can affect the entire department.

Also, abusing lenient policies can cause management to reassess those policies, which can have a negative effect on morale. It is not hard to see how absenteeism and tardiness can damage your horizontal and vertical relationships.

Absenteeism and Tardiness Will Hurt Your Career

Absenteeism and tardiness can negatively affect your career, as Nelson discovered. People judge you by your actions. An employee who is chronically late and often misses days of work may be judged to be unprofessional. Your co-workers and supervisor may feel that you are not serious about your career and your responsibilities.

Perhaps they are right. If you are often late for work or call in sick even when you are not, ask yourself why? This may be a symptom of another problem. If you can identify what it is, you will be able to correct the symptom, such as being late for work.

Do you dislike what you are doing?

Why are you risking damaging your relationships and career advancement?

Be Sure Absence Is Legitimate

Of course, there are legitimate reasons for missing work. If you are ill, it is better to stay home and recover than to force yourself to go to work where you probably will not be very efficient and where you will spread infection around the workplace. Also, emergencies arise when your family needs you.

It is not legitimate, however, to take a Monday off because your weekend schedule is too hectic to allow you to rest. Getting a jump on the weekend by calling in sick on Friday is an abuse of sick time as well.

Different companies have different policies for handling lateness, sick days, or personal time. If you work in a large company, these policies may be written down in an employee handbook. You should familiarize yourself with these guidelines. Smaller companies may not have written rules, and you will be informed of their guidelines when you are hired.

Ways to Avoid Tardiness

There are several strategies you can use to avoid tardiness and absenteeism and the damage they can do to your career.

Use weekends to relax and enjoy hobbies, but do not overschedule yourself so that Monday morning finds you exhausted and tempted to spend the day in bed.

Leave yourself plenty of time to get ready for work. This is especially important if you must get children off to school or to daycare before beginning work.

Leave extra time for the commute to work, in case of traffic tie-ups. If you know it takes 15 minutes to commute to work by 8, leaving the house at 16 minutes of 8 is not a good idea.

Keep your car in good repair, if you drive to work. Dead batteries, empty gas tanks, broken fan belts, and flat tires can often be avoided with regular maintenance.

Arrange for time off in advance to attend or prepare for special events—a wedding, your child's school play, or other personal priority. If you have a good attendance record, your request will be looked upon favorably in almost every case.

If you are experiencing serious personal problems— for example, the extended illness of a family member—you may want to see if your company has provisions for a leave of absence. Requesting a leave of absence for a legitimate reason can help you through a difficult period without straining your relationships at work.

Review

Consider the answers you gave before reading the concepts. If you feel that you understood the situation and are satisfied with your first answer, write "no change" on the line. If you feel you have new insights or understanding, write your new answer or additional information.

Is Ralph Robertson justified in criticizing Nelson?

_____

_____

What effect do Nelson's absenteeism and tardiness have on his job? On Robertson Electronics?

_____

_____

How do you think Nelson's attitude will affect the other employees?

_____

_____

Discussion

1. What impact do chronic absenteeism and tardiness have at work?

_____

_____

_____

2. What type of attitudes have contributed to your own absenteeism and tardiness?

_____

_____

3. How do you avoid absenteeism and tardiness?

_____

_____

_____

Career Plateaus

Study 17

Case Study 17
Career Plateaus

After completing this chapter, you will:

- ☐ Recognize the importance of maintaining a positive attitude during career plateaus.

- ☐ Identify several of your own strategies for maintaining a positive attitude during plateau periods.

Frank Whitman had just marked the sixth anniversary of his employment at the Hereford Insurance Company. Frank had arrived at Hereford fresh out of school filled with enthusiasm and high hopes for rapid advancement in his career. He was the youngest computer programmer in the claims department but also the most productive. For the first three years, his achievements were rewarded with steady pay raises and increased job responsibilities.

During his third year with Hereford, Frank's computer ability landed him the prestigious assignment of developing a new computer filing system for the entire claims department. The reorganization took almost one year and the results were impressive. His performance on that assignment led to a substantial pay raise, a new job title, and the promise of more challenging assignments. "Nothing can stop me now," Frank thought. "I'll be in management before I'm 30 years old."

Unfortunately, the formerly booming insurance industry had entered a period of declining profits and even large losses for some companies. Hereford, like every other major insurance supplier, was affected by this. Profits were sharply down. Major cost-saving measures went into effect.

One of those measures was the postponement—for an indefinite period—of new projects. Frank found that the assignments he had hoped to get were unavailable. At first, Frank remained a productive member of the claims department, but his job held little challenge. He missed the excitement of developing and implementing new programs.

Although Frank received his annual raise, it was much less than his previous ones. Frank felt sure that if he just had the chance to remind his supervisor of what he could do, he would be back on the fast track.

As time went on, Frank became more and more discouraged. He could see his plans for becoming a manager disappearing. It just wasn't fair, he thought. I'm losing my chance to shine because of a company policy that I had nothing to do with.

Frank's discouragement and negative attitude became obvious to his co-workers and supervisor. His personal productivity went down, and the others in his department had to work harder to pick up the slack.

Frank withdrew from the people he worked with. Going to work every morning became a chore. When one of Frank's friends suggested joining a class in advanced programming, Frank declined. "What's the use?" became Frank's standard reply to any suggestions to enhance his skills.

Your Analysis

Analyze Frank's situation. Do you think it is an unusual one?

_____

_____

What mistakes is Frank making?

_____

_____

How could Frank handle his present career plateau in a positive manner?

_____

_____

Can you predict any long-range consequences to Frank's attitude?

_____

_____

Concepts

Most people begin their careers full of high hopes and ambition. The desire to get ahead and to excel in your career is constructive. It spurs you on to do your best and increase your productivity. When your efforts are rewarded with increased responsibilities, raises, and promotions, you feel successful. Setting goals and striving to achieve them increases your prospects for career success.

When you predict your future, you may see yourself climbing the ladder of success, one rung—or even two—at a time, until you reach your goal. You may expect that your progress from rung to rung will be steady.

Plateaus Are Normal

In the real world, times of progress toward your career goal may be interspersed with plateau periods. A career plateau refers to a time when your upward progress stops and your career progress levels off. Plateaus can last from several months to several years. Few people reach their career goal without experiencing one or more plateau periods.

During a plateau, advancement stops. Have you ever dieted to take off several pounds? The first week or two of following your diet, you probably lost weight rather quickly. This encouraged you to continue; your goal was in sight. After several weeks, however, you may have reached a point where no weight came off, even though you were still faithfully following your diet. You reached a plateau. You probably felt disappointed and discouraged. You may have even given up and returned to your old eating habits.

Career plateaus also arise when you are following all the rules and your career seems to be on track. They are almost always the result of outside forces, not the result of anything you have done or not done. You may be in a company where openings for positions in management rarely arise. You may have to wait for someone to retire before you are promoted. Frank reached a career plateau as the result of conditions in the insurance industry beyond his control.

Maintain a Positive Attitude

Maintaining a positive attitude during plateaus is essential to career advancement. Good human relations skills will still be important to maintain your work relationships—perhaps more important. It is easy to project a positive attitude when life is going your way. If you can maintain that attitude in a frustrating situation, however, your efforts will be noticed and appreciated by co-workers and supervisors.

Frank's attitude may well result in hard-to-repair damage to his relationships with his co-workers. They will eventually resent having to pick up the slack. His attitude negatively affects group productivity.

How to Survive a Plateau Period

There are several strategies you can use to survive a plateau period with your attitude intact.

Remind yourself that this is not your fault.

Talk to others about what is happening.

Ask them how they handled similar situations. You are not the first person to reach a plateau, and you surely will not be the last.

Even if there is no way to change the immediate situation, talking to your boss about your long-term goals and present frustrations may help. You may receive reassurance that the plateau will be short-lived. In any event, your desire to advance will be on record. Frank has given his supervisor no clues for his change in attitude. If enough time goes by and Frank does not repair his attitude, he may seriously damage his future chances for promotion.

Use a plateau period as a time to increase your knowledge and capabilities.

A job that is not making full use of your abilities will allow you to concentrate on polishing your skills or acquiring new ones. Frank was shortsighted in turning down an opportunity to add to his computer knowledge. Do not make the same mistake. When the plateau period ends, be prepared for a higher level of responsibility.

Keep a high profile.

Contribute at meetings—you know your job well, and your ideas are important. Offer to train a new employee and share your expertise. Join the company health group, serve on the planning committee for the company picnic, or write an article for the employee newsletter. Let those in the upper echelons of your company know who you are.

Accept all challenges that come your way.

Do not turn down any assignment you feel you can handle— good performance on a difficult task can be the key to moving off that plateau.

Remember—everyone, at one time or another, gets stuck in a plateau.

Maintain your positive attitude, and use your time preparing for the day when you resume climbing that ladder toward your goal.

Review

Consider the answers you gave before reading the concepts. If you feel that you understood the situation and are satisfied with your first answer, write "no change" on the line. If you feel you have new insights or understanding, write your new answer or additional information.

Analyze Frank's situation. Do you think it is an unusual one?

_____

_____

What mistakes is Frank making?

_____

_____

How could Frank handle his present career plateau in a positive manner?

_____

_____

Can you predict any long-range consequences to Frank's attitude?

_____

_____

Discussion

1. Why is maintaining a positive attitude during a plateau
   period important?

   _____

   _____

2. List several strategies you have used for maintaining a
   positive attitude during plateaus.

   _____

   _____

   _____

3. What are some of the reasons you might experience a
   career plateau?

   _____

   _____

   _____

CAREER ADVANCEMENT

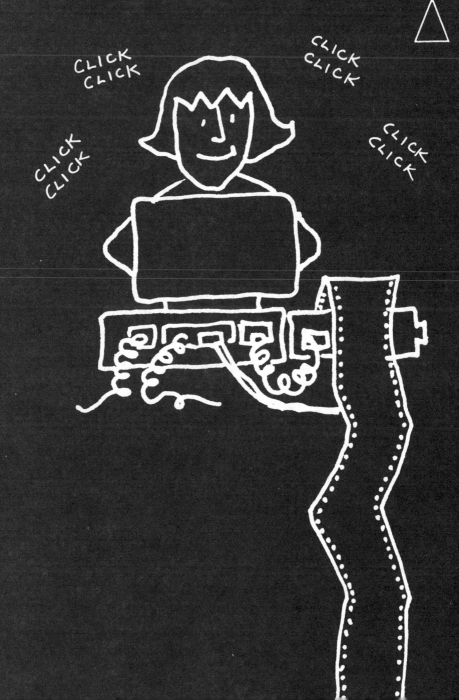

Case Study 18
Career Advancement

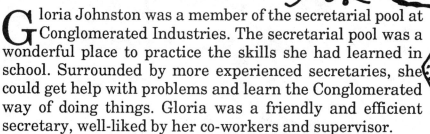

After completing this chapter, you will:

☐ Recognize the importance of a constructive attitude in career advancement.

☐ Identify behavior that will help you meet your advancement goal.

Gloria Johnston was a member of the secretarial pool at Conglomerated Industries. The secretarial pool was a wonderful place to practice the skills she had learned in school. Surrounded by more experienced secretaries, she could get help with problems and learn the Conglomerated way of doing things. Gloria was a friendly and efficient secretary, well-liked by her co-workers and supervisor.

Although she liked her job, Gloria did not want to stay in the secretarial pool forever. Some of the secretaries had been there for 20 years, but Gloria knew that was not for her. She wanted to be the secretary to a department, and eventually an executive assistant.

Gloria knew it was possible. Sharon Small had done just that. Sharon was assistant to the director of operations. Gloria had met Sharon when she delivered some work to be typed. The other secretaries told Gloria that Sharon had once been in the secretarial pool, but had quickly moved on. "A very ambitious woman. And she got that way without stepping on others," was the way Sharon was described.

Gloria decided the best way to attain her goal was to do excellent work. When she turned over work to a department, she strove to make it flawless. If there were additions and corrections, she did them promptly.

The secretarial pool was used by several departments. Each department head liked to have its letters and reports typed in a certain way. Gloria quickly realized this and made sure that the work she did was formatted correctly.

Gloria set up special formats in her computer's word processing program for the styles of letters and reports preferred by each department head. When the other secretaries noticed what a timesaver this was, she offered to help them do the same. Her supervisor appreciated Gloria's contribution to the pool's increased productivity level.

Gloria made sure that she understood how Conglomerated operated. She learned the names of the department heads and directors. She asked questions to learn what each department's role was.

Because of her work record and adaptability, Gloria was given many of the more complicated jobs. She enjoyed the challenges of typing and setting up a complex report so that it was easy to read and attractive to look at.

The operations department had a large and complex report due. Gloria was assigned to help Sharon Small prepare it. They spent two weeks working together. During that time, Sharon had an opportunity to observe Gloria's skills and attitude closely. She was impressed. Although meeting the deadline required working late several nights, Gloria did not complain. She was not afraid to speak up, offering suggestions and ideas that were well thought out and useful. Gloria reminded Sharon of herself 10 years ago.

When an opening for a department secretary in advertising needed to be filled, Sharon recommended Gloria to the department director. He was familiar with Gloria's work. His own experience, combined with the excellent references from Sharon and Gloria's supervisor, made Gloria the leading candidate for the job. When she was offered the promotion, she happily accepted.

Your Analysis

How did Gloria's attitude affect her career?

_____

_____

What specific strategies did Gloria use to advance her career?

_____

_____

Do you think Gloria will reach her goal?

_____

_____

Concepts

If you are ambitious, you want to get ahead. Some people are content with remaining in the same job, with the same level of responsibility, for their entire career. Most people, however, want to move onward and upward. They want new challenges, increased responsibility, greater status, and higher pay. These are achievable through career advancement.

Define Your Goals

The first step on the path to reaching your career goals is to define what your goals are. Examine what you want from your job. Ask yourself:

What do I want to do with my life?

What is important to me?

Where do I see myself five years from now?
Where in ten years?

Identify Realistic Steps

Once you have defined your goals, identify realistic steps to reach them. Do you have the skills needed to reach your goal? Do you need to further your education? Do you come in contact with others at work who can help you reach these goals?

Gloria knew what her goal was—to become an executive assistant. She had identified the first step on the path of reaching her goal—leaving the secretarial pool to become a department secretary. To do that, Gloria needed to demonstrate her secretarial and human relations skills.

Good job skills combined with good human relations skills are your ticket to success. You know how important a constructive attitude is to your relationships with co-workers and supervisor. It is also an important element in career advancement. Gloria would not have developed a reputation as an outstanding worker if she had merely been an excellent typist. It was the combination of her secretarial skill and her positive attitude toward work and people that assured her success.

Show Your Desire to Succeed

Make your desire to succeed visible to the people around you. This does not mean stepping on others to get ahead. It does mean projecting a cooperative attitude. Notice how Gloria shared her expertise in developing formats for reports and letters. If she had kept this to herself, she would have high personal productivity, but department productivity would not be as high as possible.

By sharing a good idea, she has increased department productivity, helped to enhance her co-workers' skills, and earned their respect and that of her supervisor. She has increased her visibility and drawn positive attention to herself and her skills.

Know Your Company

Know the company you work for. Know how it works, what each department does. Learn how your company is structured, who the department heads are, who does the hiring, firing, and promoting. Are people promoted from within the company or brought in from outside when an opening develops? Obviously, your chances to advance are greatest in a company that promotes from within.

Be Open to Opportunities

Be receptive to changes and opportunities. Gloria would have lost an excellent opportunity to show what she could do if she had turned down the assignment to work with Sharon because it required overtime. Look for opportunities to prove your ability. Do not hesitate to offer valid suggestions. People in authority welcome new ideas.

Do That Little Extra

Do a little extra. Take every opportunity to show initiative. If your goal is a management position, prepare now. Take courses in management and employee relations. Volunteer to head the department problem-solving committee.

Keep Your Positive Attitude

As you achieve your goals, do not leave your positive attitude behind. Good human relations skills are as important for supervisors as for workers—and often they are more important. Conduct yourself in such a manner that when your promotion is announced, others will be happy for you. If you find that achieving your goals involves downgrading and hurting others, perhaps it is time to reevaluate your goals.

Do all you can to make the transition a smooth one for your replacement. Volunteer to train the person who will be taking over your present job. If that is not possible, at least be sure that everything is in order. Leave an explanatory note if some aspects of the job are confusing. Jot down your new phone number, and let your replacement and supervisor know that you will be happy to answer any questions they have.

Review

Consider the answers you gave before reading the concepts. If you feel that you understood the situation and are satisfied with your first answer, write "no change" on the line. If you feel you have new insights or understanding, write your new answer or additional information.

How did Gloria's attitude affect her career?

_____

_____

What specific strategies did Gloria use to advance her career?

_____

_____

Do you think Gloria will reach her goal?

_____

_____

Discussion

1. How has a constructive attitude been important to your school or career advancement?

_____

_____

_____

2. Identify several strategies and behaviors that will help you meet your advancement goal.

_____

_____

_____

MAKING MISTAKES

Case Study 19
Making Mistakes

After completing this chapter, you will:

☐ Recognize the positive side of making mistakes.

☐ Identify strategies you used in dealing with a mistake.

Business at the Q & S Catalog Company was booming. In the last two years, annual gross sales had more than doubled. There was talk of expanding again, adding new product lines, and even expanding into Canada.

Jeremy Slezaki had literally grown up at Q & S. While in high school, he had started working in the mailroom. Back then, Q & S had employed only 10 people—including two full-time mail shippers and Jeremy. When Jeremy graduated he began working full-time.

Today, there were 20 full-time workers in the mailroom alone, and Jeremy was assistant manager. His hard work and enthusiasm impressed the shipping manager, Hannah Breck.

With Hannah's encouragement, Jeremy was attending Community College at night, majoring in business administration. Jeremy owed Hannah a lot. Over the years, she had helped him progress, giving him chances to try new things. When Jeremy was hesitant, Hannah pushed him. "Test yourself, Jeremy," she always said. "I have confidence in you—you just need confidence in yourself."

Jeremy hated to make a mistake. Of course, he did make mistakes. Hannah never belittled him, even the time when he had mailed a shipment to Portland, Maine, instead of Portland, Oregon. Her attitude made it easier for Jeremy to admit when he was wrong. And overcoming his fear of failure helped him to take on new assignments.

Monday, Hannah had told Jeremy that she was swamped with work because of the expansion plans. She was scheduled to report on the effect of new plans for the mailroom. "I've already calculated the staffing needs for 1993-1995," she told him, "but I need to prepare budget projections. And tomorrow I leave for that conference in Texas! What terrible timing. I wish I could send you to the conference to speak in my place."

"I don't think I'd be a satisfactory substitute at a 'Women in Management' seminar! I'd be happy to finish the report for you, though. I know I could do it." Jeremy had learned about formulating budget projections last semester in class.

"Jeremy, this is one time I'm not sure. You've never done this. It's important that the projections be accurate. The decision to expand will be made at Friday's meeting, based on the department reports. On the other hand, I really have no alternative. You've certainly proven your competence in other areas—all right, it's yours. Don't let me down."

Jeremy tackled the report Tuesday morning. That night, he took stacks of figures home. He worked steadily, and the budget projections were on Hannah's desk Wednesday.

Thursday morning, Jeremy was barely in the door when Hannah called him to her office. Expecting a pat on the back, Jeremy was crestfallen to hear Hannah's words. "I'm afraid the figures you used on the projected mailing costs are outdated. You didn't factor in the cost of postage increases."

Jeremy felt his face redden. "I can't imagine what I was thinking of. I'd like the chance to correct my mistake."

"Well, Jeremy, it's a good thing you got this done a day early," Hannah said. "This mistake could cost Q & S thousands in cost overruns. I know it was just an oversight. The rest of the report looks excellent. I'm confident you can fix this. Have the revised figures on my desk in the morning."

Making Mistakes   173

Your Analysis

Why do you think Jeremy made the mistake in the report?

_____

_____

Was Hannah mistaken to trust Jeremy to do the report correctly?

_____

_____

Do you think Jeremy has learned anything from his error? What and why?

_____

_____

What effect will this episode have on Jeremy's relationship with Hannah?

_____

_____

Concepts

We all make mistakes. The more you do and the harder you try, the more mistakes you will make. The only people who might not make mistakes are those who do nothing. But, of course, they are making a major mistake by doing nothing.

Admit It

Usually it is difficult to admit making a mistake. However, once you make a mistake it is better to admit it quickly, correct it if possible, and put it behind you. Fiorello La Guardia was one of the most popular and effective mayors of New York City. He was mayor during the great depression and World War II. He was an active mayor who got things done. He once said, "When I make a mistake, it's a beaut!" The people liked him for this candor.

Do Not Make Excuses

Jeremy made a mistake that, if not caught, could have proved costly. To his credit, he admitted it immediately. He did not make excuses or attempt to blame a third party. His quick apology and offer to correct his error confirm Hannah's confidence in him. Taking these actions will also restore his confidence in himself. His self-confidence is shaken, but correcting his error promptly will help fix that.

Often mistakes are well intentioned. People do the wrong thing for the right reason. They may honestly be trying to solve a problem with what they think is the best method. These kinds of mistakes are usually easier to admit to making than ones that are not so well intentioned.

Do Not Fear Making Mistakes

Fear of making mistakes can be destructive because it can paralyze you and prevent you from taking any action. If you never take a chance, if you never try something new because you fear you will make a mistake, you limit your opportunities for growth. Hannah took a chance on Jeremy; Jeremy took a chance on himself.

The outcome was that Jeremy has stretched himself, accomplishing something he had never attempted before. Because of his ability and willingness to fix his mistake, Hannah is more likely to offer Jeremy new assignments. He will continue advancing in his career.

If you are a perfectionist, you are someone who dreads making a mistake. Of course, for a human, it is very hard to do a perfect job all the time. It can prevent you from starting projects if you feel that you cannot do a perfect job. Try always to do the best you can, but be realistic.

Learn From Mistakes

You will make mistakes. The ability to learn from your mistakes and failures is important. View your mistakes as opportunities to improve.

Use Failures as Stepping-Stones

Use failure as a stepping-stone to success. Many of today's most successful entrepreneurs were unsuccessful in their first, second, third, even fourth attempts at building a business. Rather than let these failures get them down, they learned from their mistakes. They took the knowledge they gained in failing and used it to achieve success.

Try—and if you make a mistake, if you fail—try again. The only people who never make mistakes are those who never try anything new.

Review

Consider the answers you gave before reading the concepts. If you feel that you understood the situation and are satisfied with your first answer, write "no change" on the line. If you feel you have new insights or understanding, write your new answer or additional information.

Why do you think Jeremy made the mistake in the report?

_____

_____

Was Hannah mistaken to trust Jeremy to do the report correctly?

_____

_____

Do you think Jeremy has learned anything from his error? What and why?

_____

_____

What effect will this episode have on Jeremy's relationship with Hannah?

_____

_____

Discussion

1. Do you think making mistakes is always negative? Is there a positive side of making mistakes?

_____

_____

_____

2. Identify several strategies you have developed for dealing with your mistakes.

_____

_____

_____

RESTORING RELATIONSHIPS

Case Study 20
Restoring Relationships

After completing this chapter, you will:

☐ Identify mistakes that have damaged your relationships with others.

☐ Use effective strategies to repair some of your injured relationships.

Roberto Morales heaved a sigh of relief as he finished typing the last paragraph of the building proposal. It had taken one week of 12-hour days, collecting figures and writing the proposal, but now it was done.

With fewer new houses being built, Ace Construction needed to win this contract. Roberto knew that there would be layoffs if Ace did not win a major contract soon. Winning the contract for construction of the new state Motor Vehicle Inspection building would guarantee work for the next two years.

This was the first proposal Roberto had written. Being chosen to prepare such an important document was a sign of Sam Saunders' confidence in him. Of course, Roberto had wanted the job and he had let Sam know it. And the timing was perfect. Harold Washington, who would normally automatically be given the assignment, was tied up with problems at the Main Street site.

Roberto proudly placed the proposal on Sam's desk and headed outdoors for lunch. It looked like everyone was picnicking outdoors on this beautiful April day. He joined his co-workers and had just bit into his sandwich when Harold joined the group. Harold did not return his greeting, but Roberto just assumed he had not heard him. As lunch progressed, however, Roberto realized that Harold was pointedly ignoring him.

As the group returned to work, Roberto called to Harold. "Hey, Harold! I'd like a word with you." Harold turned and waited for Roberto to join him.

"What's the problem?" Roberto asked. "You were obviously ignoring me at lunch. Did I do something wrong?"

"Don't act all innocent with me!" Harold replied angrily. "I came back early today to start writing the Motor Vehicle proposal, and discovered you'd already finished it. What's the big idea? Are you trying to steal my job?"

"Hey, slow down!" Roberto was taken aback by Harold's anger. "I wasn't stealing anything from you. You were tied up at the Main Street site. I honestly didn't expect you to be back in the office at all this week. Neither did Sam. That proposal was a top priority and you know it."

"Well, you certainly didn't waste any time taking over," Harold countered.

"Of course I was happy to get the assignment. After all, I've been helping you prepare proposals for months now. And you've been a great teacher. Don't you think it was time for me to be given more responsibility? Don't you think I can handle it?" Roberto said. "Believe me, Harold, I'm not trying to steal your job. You're Sam's right-hand man and we all know it."

"I'm not sure you're ready for such a big responsibility," Harold said. "But maybe you're right. I guess I should've talked to you first." It was not exactly an apology, but Roberto offered his hand in truce. The two men shook hands and walked inside.

Your Analysis

Analyze the situation. What human relations mistakes are illustrated in Case Study 20?

_____

_____

Has the relationship between Roberto and Harold been seriously injured?

_____

_____

Have Roberto and Harold repaired their relationship?

_____

_____

What do you think will happen as a result of the day's events?

_____

_____

Concepts

Correcting a mistake on paper is much easier than correcting the damage to a relationship. However, in the long run, repairing injured relationships and soothing ruffled feathers may be more important to your future. Conflicts, both on the job and off, are inevitable. Misunderstandings and arguments can permanently damage your relationships with your co-workers or supervisor if you allow them to go unrepaired.

The Dangers of Not Acting

Harold has jumped to a wrong conclusion about Roberto's motives. He feels threatened and afraid that Roberto is trying to steal his job. Can you imagine the relationship between Harold and Roberto if they had not talked?

Several things can happen if your relationships are injured and allowed to go unrepaired:

You can become preoccupied with the problem.

You may find yourself replaying the scene over and over in your head. You may recall everything a particular person has ever said to you, analyzing it for slights or insults. Dwelling on a problem steals time that could be used productively.

Like a toothache, an unresolved problem is always there, reminding you of its presence when you'd rather be thinking of something else.

Injured relationships add to the stress already present in the workplace.

Long hours, a heavy workload, and complicated job responsibilities are compounded by the stress of working with someone who is angry at you.

Damaged relationships can jeopardize your career.

If you are unable to work with a co-worker because of a damaged relationship, your personal productivity—and the productivity of your group—will be affected.

It is possible to become a victim as the result of a conflict with an employee or a supervisor.

Imagine what would happen if the bad feelings between Harold and Roberto were left unchecked. Harold could seriously undermine Roberto's career. In the future, he could dwell on mistakes Roberto makes and suggest to Sam that Roberto is not ready for extra responsibility.

The Value of Good Relationships

Roberto will learn much more if he has a good relationship with Harold. Harold has the knowledge and expertise in proposal writing that Roberto needs if he is to get ahead. Harold could act as a mentor to Roberto, showing him the ropes.

Roberto is not the only person with something to gain from a strong relationship. Harold will also further his own career by building a strong relationship with Roberto. He will be availing himself of Roberto's fresh ideas and a new perspective on a problem. Working with Roberto, he can demonstrate his leadership ability to Sam. The productivity of Roberto and Harold combined may be much greater than the sum of their individual efforts. Of course, there is also the advantage of working in an environment where you are liked and respected.

When two people are joined in a relationship that has advantages for both, it is a mutually rewarding relationship. Both parties benefit from cooperation.

Act Promptly

Resolve to act promptly to restore injured relationships. Even if you are not responsible for the misunderstanding, take the initiative to repair it. Roberto's prompt action helped to resolve Harold's misunderstanding.

Permit others to repair relationships with you. Do not give in to wounded feelings or nurse minor misunderstandings into major problems. To his credit, Harold listens to Roberto's explanation and allows the healing process to begin.

In your dealings with others, resolve not to leap to conclusions. Do not always look for a negative explanation for another's behavior. Remember—like you, your co-workers and your supervisor are only human. Advancement in your career may very well depend on your ability to repair injured relationships.

Review

Consider the answers you gave before reading the concepts. If you feel that you understood the situation and are satisfied with your first answer, write "no change" on the line. If you feel you have new insights or understanding, write your new answer or additional information.

Analyze the situation. What human relations mistakes are illustrated in Case Study 20?

_____

_____

Has the relationship between Roberto and Harold been seriously injured?

_____

_____

Have Roberto and Harold repaired their relationship?

_____

_____

What do you think will happen as a result of the day's events?

_____

_____

Discussion

1. Identify some traits in your behavior that have damaged your relationships with others.

_____

_____

_____

2. What strategies can you use to repair injured relationships?

_____

_____

_____

DEALING WITH CRITICISM

Case Study 21
Dealing With Criticism

After completing this chapter, you will:

☐ Recognize why constructive criticism is important.

☐ Identify ways by which you have benefited from criticism.

A rt class was Gary Major's favorite subject. He had natural talent, and his parents and teachers encouraged his efforts. He believed that art was a talent, not a skill that could be taught.

To some extent, he was right. What Gary did not understand was that artists needed to understand the theory and technique of drawing and painting if they were to improve.

His high school fine arts teacher was a firm believer in the value of learning technique. His teaching and grading system reflected that belief. Gary did not excel in those classes because he rejected his teacher's comments on ways to improve his pictures. Gary could not tolerate criticism of his artwork. He took any criticism as a personal insult, a statement that he had no talent.

Gary had his heart set on attending a prestigious New York art academy. The cost was staggering; Gary, however, was convinced that he would be awarded a scholarship. He confidently sent his work to the review committee.

Gary was stunned when his scholarship bid was rejected. He was even more infuriated by the comments he received in explanation—some talent, no knowledge of technique, needs improvement. "Those big city art snobs can't even recognize talent when they see it!" he fumed.

After spending the summer moping around the house, Gary applied for the position of drafting apprentice at the airplane manufacturing plant where his father worked. Gary was hired and attended the three-month training course. To his surprise, he liked drafting. He liked the detail work, the need for precision and accuracy. In a way, it was like being an artist, only he was sketching airplane parts instead of still lifes.

Gary trained with a veteran drafter for one year. He was not given great responsibility, but he was learning his trade. For the first time, Gary could accept criticism of his work. After all, he reasoned, I'm just an apprentice. I'm supposed to be learning and making mistakes.

When his apprenticeship period ended, Gary was assigned to the electrical department. Now Gary was given jobs to do on his own. If there was a problem with one of his drawings, the designers and engineers would discuss it with him. Unfortunately, Gary's problems with criticism resurfaced. Because he was now a full-fledged drafter, he felt that he knew all there was to know about drafting. He thought criticism of his work was a sign that he had failed.

Gary resented any criticism at all, no matter how well-meant. If someone questioned his placement of a wire or the type of outlet he had drawn, he sulked for the rest of the day. He was quickly earning a reputation as a troublesome member of the department.

Collaboration with other drafters was almost impossible. If his ideas were not used, he took it as an implied criticism of his talent and skill. There were some people in the department Gary refused to talk to at all because they had changed his drawings.

After Gary had worked as a drafter for 18 months, his boss was forced to cut the staff. Although there were others with less experience, Gary was let go.

Your Analysis

How would you characterize Gary's feelings about criticism?

_____

_____

Do you think the criticism by Gary's art teachers and co-workers was constructive or destructive?

_____

_____

How could Gary have benefited from the criticism?

_____

_____

Concepts

Everyone has faced criticism at one time or another. It's impossible to escape it at home or at work. You can be criticized for your attitude, your appearance, or your lack of skill in certain areas.

Being able to accept criticism and to learn from it is an important human relations skill.

Criticism Often Hurts

Often, criticism hurts. You do not like to hear that you or something you have done needs improvement. Everyone likes to think of herself or himself as competent in all areas. Of course, no one can know everything; no one can look wonderful everyday; no one can project a positive attitude at all times; and no one is talented or skilled in every area. Criticism is inevitable.

Constructive Criticism Helps You Learn

Criticism can be a learning experience if given constructively. Constructive criticism is criticism given to help you learn.

Gary's art teacher offered him constructive criticism. He recognized Gary's talent and wanted to help him acquire the technical skills that would improve his work.

Unfortunately, Gary's ego and defensive attitude prevent him from benefiting from his teacher's criticism. He is unable to accept it as well-meaning advice; instead, Gary interprets the criticism as a personal attack.

Gary would be justified in his reaction if the criticism were intended to hurt. Imagine Gary's reaction if his teacher had said, "Whatever made you think you were an artist? Look at this dreadful drawing! Haven't you ever heard of perspective?"

Avoid Destructive Criticism

Criticism intended to inflict hurt is destructive criticism. It does not offer Gary any way to improve his work. It's intention is to wound, not teach.

Constructive criticism is not presented in anger or as a criticism of you personally. Imagine that Gary's teacher criticized his work this way: "Gary, I like the subject matter you've chosen, and this painting shows that you have talent. I see you're having a problem with the perspective. Why don't you review the techniques in Chapter 12 of the text."

Gary never learned to accept criticism and learn from his mistakes. Ultimately, it cost him his job. Although he has good drafting ability, his destructive attitude toward criticism interfered in his relationships at work.

When You Criticize Others

You will not always be in the position of accepting criticism. Sometimes, you will find yourself directing critical remarks at a co-worker.

It is important to remember—no one learns from destructive criticism.

Be sure the criticism you offer is constructive.

If you are angry, give yourself time to calm down.

Do not let criticism become a personal attack.

Put yourself in the other person's place, and only give criticism the way you would like it given to you.

Review

Consider the answers you gave before reading the concepts. If you feel that you understood the situation and are satisfied with your first answer, write "no change" on the line. If you feel you have new insights or understanding, write your new answer or additional information.

How would you characterize Gary's feelings about criticism?

_____

_____

Do you think the criticism by Gary's art teachers and co-workers was constructive or destructive?

_____

_____

How could Gary have benefited from the criticism?

_____

_____

Discussion

1. What is meant by constructive criticism?

_____

_____

_____

2. Identify ways by which you have benefited from criticism.

_____

_____

_____

Case Study 22
Leaving a Job

After completing this chapter, you will:

- ☐ Recognize that leaving a particular job may be the right decision.

- ☐ Recognize the importance of leaving a job in a positive manner.

- ☐ Identify ways to leave a job in a positive manner.

- ☐ Identify how you felt when you left a course or a job in a positive manner.

Walter Higgins had worked at Steinman Brothers Accounting Services 12 years. It was like a second home for him. Morris Steinman and his brother, Marvin, had given him his first job after graduation, and he felt a deep loyalty to them.

Walter began as the assistant to the head bookkeeper, Salvatore. The frequent contact Walter had with the accountants on staff helped him realize that he wanted to be an accountant also. Within a year, he began attending night school to earn an accounting degree.

Everyone knew that Walter was attending school. He received support and encouragement from them all, including Morris and Marvin. "Work hard and you will succeed, Walter," they told him. "There is a good future for you at Steinman's."

Walter's diligence earned him high marks at school and advancement at work. He was promoted to head bookkeeper when Salvatore retired.

Just before his graduation, Morris and Marvin called Walter into their office. "Walter," they told him, "we want you to start training Deirdre as your replacement. After all, you'll soon be an accountant. We can't have you stuck in the bookkeeping department! We've been short one accountant, as you know. The job is yours if you want it."

Walter was a good accountant. He enjoyed his work—it was challenging and interesting. After six months, he decided to become a CPA, a certified public accountant. That was the top of his profession. Morris and Marvin were CPAs, as were their three senior accountants.

Walter went back to night school to prepare for the CPA exam. It was a tough exam, but Walter passed on his first try. His co-workers threw him a surprise party the day he received his license.

Walter learned all aspects of accounting. That was one advantage to working for a small firm. As time went on, however, Walter realized that his job had become static. He was not progressing. Although he received a yearly pay raise, he wanted more responsibility.

He asked Morris and Marvin about chances for advancement. They listened intently and praised his work and his initiative. Unfortunately, he was their youngest accountant. It would be years before he would be able to take over larger accounts. They told Walter they understood his frustration, but added, "You're young yet. Be patient, Walter."

Walter spoke to his friend Charles. Charles helped him verbalize his career goals. Charles pointed out that, as much as Walter liked his co-workers and his bosses, he needed to take steps to fulfill his desire for more responsibility. Walter told Charles that a CPA position was being advertised at a large local firm with a reputation for providing opportunity for advancement. Walter asked Charles for his advice.

Your Analysis

If you were Charles, what advice would you give to Walter?

_____

_____

If Walter decides to leave Steinman's, why is it important for him to leave in a positive way?

_____

_____

How can Walter accomplish a positive departure?

_____

_____

Concepts

You may spend your career working for the same company in the same position. Chances are, however, that you will work for several different firms during your career. Knowing when to move on and how to depart in a positive manner can ease the transition, for you and for your present employer.

Knowing When to Leave

Walter has to face the fact that it is time to leave Steinman's if he is to achieve his career goal. He is obviously highly motivated to improve himself and succeed. He has shown that he can set goals and meet them, even if it takes several years. He has even identified his problem and talked it over with Morris and Marvin.

If he decided to stay at Steinman's from a sense of gratitude or loyalty, or because it is a familiar, comfortable environment, it would be a mistake. Eventually, his dissatisfaction and frustration could undermine his positive attitude toward his job.

Walter has done his best for the firm by being a productive employee for many years. He would happily remain there if he could accomplish his goals, but the reality is that it will be years before that would be possible. It is time to move on.

The same dilemma confronts many workers who are faced with a choice between the safe, comfortable, familiar job they have now and the chance to challenge themselves and advance their careers by moving on.

How will you know if you should change jobs? It will be an easy decision if you are unhappy in your present position. Perhaps you would prefer to be in a small firm and are in a large one, or vice versa. Maybe you are practicing the wrong career for you. Walter decided early in his career that he wanted to be an accountant, not a bookkeeper. He was lucky to be able to change his occupation and remain with a firm he liked.

Analyze Your Reasons

Analyze why you are unhappy with your job. If it is because of a personality conflict, try to resolve it through communication with the appropriate people. It is rarely a good idea to leave a job because of a personality conflict.

If the problem stems from the negative attitude of a co-worker or supervisor, a third party may be helpful in resolving the problem.

If the problem stems from a destructive attitude on your part, though, changing jobs will almost never help. The problem will travel with you if you do not take steps to correct it.

Sometimes, as in Walter's case, you must leave because you have reached the highest level you can in a particular job. There are no opportunities for advancement in sight. Be sure that you have explored all your options before taking any major step, however. Talk to your supervisor. Be honest about your reasons for considering leaving. You may discover that the opportunity you seek will be opening up soon.

Leave in a Positive Way

Once you have made your decision, leave your job in a positive way. Keep your productivity level high even while job hunting. Your present employer is still your priority.

When you have accepted another job, resign in person. Tell your supervisor or the personnel department your reasons for leaving. Give plenty of notice—two weeks is traditional, although some firms request three to four weeks. During this time, do not let your job performance slip. Offer to train your replacement. Even if your offer is not accepted, it will be appreciated.

Resist the urge to make negative comments about your co-workers, supervisor, or the company. Do not make unfavorable comparisons between your present job and your new one. Leave on a positive note, and you will keep all your future options open. Remember, someday you may want to return to the same company.

Sometimes, the choice to leave a job is not your own. You may be laid off for reasons beyond your control. When this happens, it is hard not to feel bitter. It is normal to experience anger or even grief when you lose your job. If that happens, it is more important than ever to leave in a positive way. Do not spoil an exemplary working record with words spoken in anger.

Remember that being laid off is not a reflection of your performance. Most often, it is caused by economic problems facing the company, many times as a result of things beyond its control. Sometimes, productive workers are laid off because of rules governing seniority.

Losing your job is even more serious if you lose your positive attitude with it. That will hamper your efforts to find a new job or your chances of being recalled when conditions improve.

Review

Consider the answers you gave before reading the concepts. If you feel that you understood the situation and are satisfied with your first answer, write "no change" on the line. If you feel you have new insights or understanding, write your new answer or additional information.

If you were Charles, what advice would you give to Walter?

_____

_____

If Walter decides to leave Steinman's, why is it important for him to leave in a positive way?

_____

_____

How can Walter accomplish a positive departure?

_____

_____

Discussion

1. When could leaving your present job be the right decision?

   _____

   _____

   _____

2. List several important points to remember when you decide to resign.

   _____

   _____

   _____

3. Identify a time when it was important to leave a course or a job in a positive manner.

   _____

   _____

Index

career, 201
company, 78
grammar, 105
gratitude, 201
grief, 203
grievance, 78
gripe, 50
group, 32, 49-50, 67-68, 87, 132,
    135-137, 157
    morale, 70
growth, 176
grudge, 32
guidelines, 146

H

habit, 125, 155
handbook, 146
    employee, 136
healing process, 185
health, 127, 157
hierarchy, 135
hobbies, 80, 147
honesty, 115-116
human relations, 6, 10, 13, 15,
    23, 97-98
    good, 6, 23, 50
human relations skill, 5, 59, 94,
    97, 107, 115-116, 120, 135,
    156, 165, 193
human relations skills, 123, 167
human relationships, 10
humor, 126

I

ill, 146
illness, 147
infection, 146
information, 68, 87, 89
    confidential, 88
    sharing, 24
initiation, 135, 137
initiative, 116, 126, 167, 185
insult, 183

integrity
    personal, 116
interest, 59, 87, 124
intruder, 135

J

jargon, 105
jealousy, 42
job, 15, 23, 31, 41, 49-51, 56, 59,
    67-70, 77-78, 80, 84, 87-89,
    105, 107, 115-116, 123-126,
    135-136, 142, 145, 157, 165,
    167, 176, 183, 194, 198, 201-203
    perfect, 123
    performance, 67, 127
    responsibilities, 41
    satisfaction, 64, 67
job description, 41
job hunting, 202
job satisfaction, 68
job security, 31, 42
job skill, 165
journal, 79

K

knowledge, 68, 98, 157, 176, 184
    common, 88

L

laid off, 203
late, 145-146
lateness, 146
learn, 135-136
leave of absence, 147
lecture, 106
listening, 5, 106, 125
loyalty, 88-89, 115-116, 201
    personal, 115

M

management, 167
manager, 41
mentor, 42, 184
message, 87